KELLY BROOK

Close Up

The Autobiography

Sidgwick & Jackson

First published 2014 by Sidgwick & Jackson
an imprint of Pan Macmillan, a division of Macmillan Publishers Limited
Pan Macmillan, 20 New Wharf Road, London N1 9RR
Basingstoke and Oxford
Associated companies throughout the world
www.panmacmillan.com

ISBN 978-0-283-07199-7 (HB)
ISBN 978-0-283-07213-0 (TPB)

1 3 5 7 9 8 6 4 2

A CIP catalogue record for this book is available from the British Library.

Typeset by Ellipsis Digital Limited, Glasgow
Printed and bound by CPI Group (UK) Ltd, Croydon, CR0 4YY

Visit www.panmacmillan.com to read more about all our books
and to buy them. You will also find features, author interviews and
news of any author events, and you can sign up for e-newsletters
so that you're always first to hear about our new releases.

I have often wondered where I would be without my boobs. They are a very prominent 30 FF and in a strange way they have defined my life over the past twenty years. They've brought fun, opportunity, attention and drama. They've been misunderstood, exploited, loved and admired, ridiculed and humiliated. I thought it only appropriate to dedicate my first autobiography to THEM. Let's face it, they have created far more headlines than any rugby player or A-list Hollywood movie star that I have dated, more than any sacking from a mainstream TV show, or any film that I have actually starred in. If anything, they have been the most consistently spoken about thing in my career. I have basically built an empire around them. They are my loyal friends!

Contents

I

The End

January 2007

That week was crazy. It was pilot season in Los Angeles and I was going from audition to audition, juggling callbacks, driving to meetings, on the phone to my agent. I'd just been asked to test for a US TV show called *Samantha Who?* for ABC. Life was exciting. Things were happening. Billy Zane and I were engaged and living in a stunning Spanish duplex apartment in Hancock Park, a pretty, sleepy, bohemian part of LA, where the houses were old and the streets were leafy. I was exactly where I wanted to be.

Billy was directing a film, *RedLine*, on the Paramount lot just down the road, and I was at home when my mum called. I was immediately worried. Not because I had a sixth sense or anything, but because she rarely called during the week, and if she did, it was bad news.

'Kelly?' Her voice sounded anxious. I sat down.

'I have something to tell you.' She paused. She was clearly very upset. 'Your dad has been to the doctor's about those lumps in his neck and they are calling us back in to the hospital.'

Lumps in his neck? It didn't sound good. A couple of years earlier, my dad had had a cyst removed from his neck, but I'd always thought he was fine. He was a fifty-seven-year-old scaffolder from Kent, the sort of bloke who was always fine. He was a rock. He drank like a fish and smoked like a chimney, but nothing touched the sides. He would be back at work the next day, laughing with his mates, still cracking the same old jokes. But it turned out my mother had been worried about his health for a while. She had originally put his pale skin and thin frame down to the fact it was winter and he was working hard. But then my dad had started to complain about having trouble swallowing. There was something pressing on his oesophagus and it had worried my mother enough for her to do some online research. Over the course of a few days, she had begun to suspect non-Hodgkin lymphoma, an aggressive form of cancer that affects the lymph nodes. They were due to go to the hospital for a biopsy the following day.

I was in shock. I knew my parents were heavy drinkers and smokers – everyone was where we lived – but I wasn't expecting this. I immediately telephoned my friend Mina, who'd had ovarian cancer and had come out the other side. She was a health food fiend who believed in alternative cures and that eating properly, loading up on macrobiotic food and looking after yourself was the way to beat cancer. And she was living proof. So I called and explained my father's condition and she put me at ease. He could get through this, she said, but the biopsy would be very dangerous and would multiply the cancer cells, so my father must drink miso soup to stop the internal bleeding. I called my parents back immediately to tell them this, and suggested to my dad, as advised by Mina, that he soak kombu seaweed and cabbage together to form a sort of poultice and wrap it round his neck to reduce the cyst or tumour. I'm pretty sure my parents must have thought I was certifiable when I finally put down the phone.

I knew I'd gone all hippy-dippy LA. In fact, the full-blown total hippy-dippy LA with tantric bells on. But I couldn't help it. I think it was panic. I felt powerless: I was miles away from home, I couldn't do anything, and I didn't like it. I am not that sort of person. I always fix things. I am the go-to fixer in our family. So instead of doing nothing, having a cry and trying to come to terms with the situation, I sprang into action. I ordered packets of miso online and I went shopping at Erewhon – the organic and natural food store – for the kind of supplies I'd need if I was going to get Dad to go 'alternative'.

Next, I blew out the auditions, cancelled my call-backs, sent my apologies to the studio, called up Billy on set and told him the situation, then booked myself on the first flight home.

Just as I was boarding, my mother called to say the biopsy had gone well but they had seen a speck on the X-ray of Dad's lung. They weren't sure if it was malignant, but they'd know more on Friday, when they would get the test results back.

I flew on the Thursday and landed on the Friday morning with a suitcase full of wholegrains, seaweed, cabbage, miso soup, twig tea and rice syrups. Surely, I determined as I battled my way out of Heathrow, my parents had to wake up and realize it was time to eat more healthily, to stop the drinking and the smoking and exercise a little? It was not much of a sacrifice when you considered the rewards.

My brother, Damian, and his girlfriend, also called Kelly, were about to have a beautiful baby girl, and they already had Thomas, who was nearly two. What a joy to watch your grandchildren grow and share with them all you knew. Not only that but Damian had just returned after a year in Afghanistan, where he had been based in Helmand, one of the most dangerous regions of the country. There was so much to celebrate: a son returning home safe from war, the arrival of their first grand-daughter, and I was planning my wedding and had just bought a beautiful farmhouse twenty minutes from their home. I had been living in LA for a number of years, but after my nephew had been born, I'd decided to move back. My mother had been deeply worried about my brother during those months he was in Afghanistan and I felt the family needed me around a little bit more.

As soon as I got home I dumped my suitcase and drove like the crazy woman I clearly was to my parents' house, where they were waiting along with my brother. My mother was so anxious that when I arrived she was already sitting in the car, ready to go to the hospital to get the test results.

I remember thinking there was such negative energy in the hospital and being shocked at the expression on my parents' faces; they had always been so strong and invincible, and now they both looked sick and grey with worry. It was the hardest experience of my life, and as I sat down in the doctor's office, I nearly burst into tears.

The doctor was an odd man who, in that typically British stiff-upper-lipped way, tried to be light-hearted. My dad joined in and they shared a couple of simply hilarious jokes. The doctor informed us the biopsy had come up clear and there was no sign of cancer in the lymph nodes, but before we all had a chance to exhale, he carried on, saying my dad's condition was very serious and he was worried the speck on his lung could potentially be cancerous. My poor mum started to cry, while my father looked on in shock. It was so upsetting, and I could see my brother, who had been through so much already, trying to hold it together. The doctor wanted to do a biopsy of my dad's lung. This would involve puncturing it. I was horrified. If he suspected my dad's lung was sick, why would he perform such a serious procedure?

I was on the verge of suggesting something else, something alternative, but I could see I'd get short shrift. My parents are of the generation that believes everything they are told by men in white coats; my LA ideas would only irritate them. On the way out, a nurse handed my mother a pamphlet full of helpline numbers and other information on how they could apply for sickness benefits. I know it was meant to be helpful, but it felt like they were saying he should just give up. There was not an ounce of positivity in that place.

I drove to my parents' house, and while they went to the pub, I cooked up miso soup with shiitake mushrooms and spring onions, and baked some fresh salmon. I boiled brown rice and added sautéed onions; I was desperate for them to like the food. I'd been online and found local organic markets and bought them cookery books so they could start thinking about eating a bit better. I went into my mum's fridge and saw the usual blocks of cheese, pink sausages, white bread, marg and industrial-size packets of streaky bacon. I immediately wanted to chuck it all away, but I knew this would not make me popular.

A few hours later, they rolled in. My dad was pretty drunk, so I handed him a non-alcoholic Beck's, as he wouldn't know the difference. Dinner was ruined, but I managed to salvage what I could. We all sat down, and because my dad was tipsy, he started to mimic the guy from *Masterchef*, critiquing every mouthful. It was hilarious. The more laughs he got, the more he ate, so I didn't mind at all. Apparently, his friends in the pub had been teasing him and telling him not to worry, saying if anything were to happen to him, they'd look after my mum. My mum told me this, adding, 'If that's not a good enough reason for your dad to live, I don't know what is.'

The next day, he got up at 6 a.m. with a hangover to go to work. I went downstairs and suggested maybe he should take the day off, but he replied his friend was picking him up in fifteen minutes. I think he just wanted to get back to normal. He cursed me for giving him 'that Beck's' as he felt properly dreadful. I chuckled, as I knew it had no bloody alcohol in it. I made him some twig tea and had just started heating the brown rice from the night before, adding some raisins and rice honey to sweeten it, when my dad snuck off. As he was getting into his truck, I ran out in my dressing gown to give it to him.

'Dad, you forgot your breakfast,' I shouted. He wasn't going to get away that easily.

For the next few days my parents came to stay in my farmhouse in the Kent countryside, where I tempted them with healthy soups made from local produce. We took walks in the orchard and played with Thomas and just savoured every moment. I don't know how I did it, but I even managed to convince my father to come to a yoga class. It was hatha yoga and I told him it would be very relaxing and calming, and was something we could do together. He came once and spent most of the lesson chanting 'om's and being quite a distance from his toes.

Naturally, I then bought the whole family crystals, explaining to them what each of the crystals did and how they could have healing properties. I was on an evangelical LA mission to educate them on alternative methods of healing, whether they wanted to listen or not. And I am pretty sure they were humouring me. During that week, I was going up to London to work on my first lingerie designs with New Look, but I called them every day to see what they were eating. I drove my mum nuts; I am sure they lied on a couple of occasions just to shut me up. It was a lot for everyone to take in, particularly for my father, who had to face the prospect of not working again, which was not only a financial worry but also a great loss, as he loved his job and his work colleagues more than anything. It was the only thing he'd ever known.

On the day of his biopsy, I sent him some flowers and I went straight round to their house after work. Dad did not look good at all. The doctor had had to go into his lung twice, causing it to collapse by 30 per cent. But that was the least of it. The results came back fairly swiftly. My dad had non-small cell lung cancer, probably caused by smoking.

'How long have I got?' asked my dad, when the doctor delivered the news forty-eight hours later.

'Six months,' came the reply.

'That's a bummer,' declared Dad, as we walked out of the hospital. 'I've just taxed the car.'

We all laughed. Typical Dad!

On the way home, I suggested that before Dad started treatment, we should all take a trip. My dad couldn't fly because of his collapsed lung, so the options were limited. But it would be a positive thing to do, to spend some time together as a family, and I offered to organize a wonderful weekend break in Paris, when we could visit the sights together and then pop over to Brussels to see my aunt, my mum's sister, who lives there.

While we were away, I asked my gardener to plant some vegetables and herbs in the garden so we'd be able to cook Dad some delicious soups later in the year. I had this fantasy that I could imbue the vegetables from my garden with cancer-curing properties if I spoke or sang to them – much like in the film *Like Water for Chocolate*. If I filled them with cancer-curing thoughts, then that's just what they'd do. It sounds desperate, because I was. People do and believe in all sorts of extraordinary things when they are trying to save the life of someone they love. They'll do anything, try anything in the hope that it makes a difference. And I was on a mission. I was trying to bring as much light, love and positivity to the situation as possible. My dad and mum had so much to cope with, I thought the way I could best help everyone was by staying upbeat. I even thanked the cancer for making us take the trip to Paris in the first place! If Dad hadn't got cancer we wouldn't have spent quality time together as a family, visiting some beautiful places and creating some lovely memories, so in a funny way I am grateful.

Paris was fabulous. We went to Sacré-Coeur and walked under the stunning arches at Notre-Dame; we travelled out to Giverny to wonder at Monet's beautiful gardens, where he painted some of his most famous works including *Water Lilies*. Then we went to Belgium to visit my aunt and decided to go shopping. My dad was looking a bit scruffy and was feeling very tired; his lung was not yet fully inflated and it was a huge strain to breathe. I dragged him into Hugo Boss and immediately demanded he buy the most 'macking' suit he could find. He was so reluctant, so exhausted that I had to force him. I picked out a wonderful grey pinstripe with pink lining and a beautiful salmon-pink shirt. He looked so handsome, and the suit fitted like a glove. We stepped out of the shop and all of a sudden, instead of walking thirty paces behind, he was striding ahead of all of us looking the bee's knees.

'Dad!' I shouted after him. 'Every time you go to the hospital now, you need to dress in your new suit looking like you mean business and you're not a patient.'

And he did. Every time he went for checks or chemo, my father popped on his Hugo Boss. It made him feel better.

When we got back to the UK, Dad's work friends threw him a leaving party at the local pub. However much he'd wanted to keep working, it just wouldn't have been possible, especially once his treatment started. His friends awarded him a scaffolding spanner they'd hand-dipped in gold and engraved with the words 'Ken Parsons, Best Scaffolder in the World'. I think my dad was tickled pink. They had all also chipped in to give him some money as a leaving present. My dad was so moved his eyes welled up and I thought he was going to cry, until one of his mates yelled, 'Ken! You'd better not cry in here or we will give you something to really cry about.'

By the end of the evening they were all plastered, and one of the younger scaffolders was crying, saying he'd miss my dad, which was a little ironic as my dad had wound him up hugely on the site. The poor young man once threatened to knock him out cold. But Dad's spirits were really buoyed and he was touched by the generosity of all his colleagues and friends. I think when a life-changing event like cancer comes along, you realize just how much you're loved.

Over the next few weeks my dad began his cancer treatment. The chemo didn't make him feel sick at all, but the steroids kept him awake at night. The following weekend was Mother's Day, and on the Friday before, my brother's girlfriend gave birth to a baby girl, Millie. There was so much to celebrate and I hosted a wonderful after-noon tea with scones and clotted cream, sandwiches, dressed crab and all sorts of hams and cheeses. Not exactly macrobiotic, but I allowed my parents to cheat! The whole family came, and I covered the house in daffodils and ordered fifty pink and white balloons.

Between hospital appointments, Dad was desperate to keep busy, so over the coming weeks he would visit my house and do odd jobs: rebuilding the pagoda, cleaning the pool and keeping an eye on all the workers who were coming and going, making sure they were doing what they were supposed to. I ordered some easels and paints and would cook lunch or dinner while my dad worked or painted in the garden. Sometimes he and Mum would come and stay for a few days if they wanted a break. My house was only ten minutes from the hospital so it was handy when he was having treatment.

We'd frequent different village pubs in Kent – Mum, Dad, me and now Billy who'd come to stay. My dad loved the Who'd a Thought It, where they have great food and serve all day; plus they serve champagne by the glass. One hot, sunny, lazy afternoon, we lucked out, as the landlord was wine-tasting, so we stayed all afternoon tasting a variety of Merlots and Pinots accompanied by chocolate mousse and fine cheese. It was heavenly and we all felt like we were on holiday.

I got so much joy from those days as we spent quality time together, doing what we loved. Billy loved the movies, so he took my dad to see *300*, about the Spartans and the Persians, a story my dad often spoke about. It amazed me how much energy my dad had that at every opportunity he wanted to do something. There was no sitting back and feeling sorry for himself. I remember one day I decided I wanted water lilies in my pond, so he immediately drove me to a nursery where they were farmed and bought some.

I also remember ordering a fridge-freezer for the pool house. I got a call early one morning from the deliverymen asking where they should go. It was 8 a.m., so I told them to meet me in the orchard and I would be up there in a couple of minutes. After clocking that they had to lift it a few metres up the hill, they told me they only had a five-minute window to deliver the fridge and my time was rapidly running out. By the time I got out of the house, they'd flown, leaving a six-foot fridge-freezer in the middle of the garden. I complained to my dad, and then I complained to the store and was put through to various departments. When I hung up, Dad called me from his mobile and told me to meet him at the pool house. He had only lifted the massive fridge on his own, put it on his pickup truck and hauled it round. He'd put those horrid, lazy deliverymen who were fighting fit and the right side of forty to shame. My dad the hero.

Dad had a few sick days while on the meds and hated having to go to the hospital. However, he did befriend an old flame of his brother's, who was always on hand. She worked at the hospital and was continually checking in on him. I would wind up Mum about how lovely she was and how attentive. Mum didn't find it very funny.

In the end, when it was clear the chemo hadn't worked, the doctor suggested radiation therapy. Dad would have to wait three weeks before he could start. He was extremely miserable at this point and wasn't taking anything short of a miraculous recovery well. I had to do something. He couldn't sit around on his own feeling depressed for three weeks; it would not be good for him. So I booked both of my parents flights to LA. Normally, it was my mum who refused to go anywhere, but this time it was my dad who freaked. I think it was all a little too much for him. But I was not taking no for an answer.

LA was fabulous. We ate at the Little Door, a cute French restaurant on 3rd Street. We had meatballs with some old mates of mine; we ate fish at the glamorous Ivy at The Shore and visited Malibu and Venice Beach, hanging out with hunky surfers at Paradise Cove. We flew by helicopter from Little Pedro's to Catalina Island. My dad had manicures, reiki, massages and pedicures. It was fantastic. We were only there for ten days, but it felt longer. My friends were wonderful, and my parents loved it. Weeks after we got back, they were still on a high.

The radiation treatment was intense. It was ten minutes every day, and some days my dad was so very ill he said he felt like he'd been sunburned from the inside. However, on his good days, he spoke about going back to work and we all hoped he would, as he loved it so much.

On one of his sick days, Billy bought him a bunch of self-help cancer DVDs, which they tried to watch together, but one of the DVDs got stuck in the player and he couldn't get the thing out. Dad used every tool imaginable trying to rescue it, but he failed, and as he told me the story, I roared with laughter and said, 'Dad, you're the unluckiest man I have ever known. When are you going to get a break?'

Anyone who has ever been in the desperate, miserable situation of watching a parent die will tell you that you take comfort from the stupid jokes about stuck DVDs, paying too much car tax and force-feeding them macrobiotic food. The little rays of sunshine help and sometimes manifest themselves in the weirdest of ways.

So when I was asked if I wanted to take part in *Strictly Come Dancing*, I grabbed the opportunity with both hands. It may sound odd to say I was saved by *Strictly Come Dancing* – in fact, it probably sounds completely fatuous – but it is true. Not only did it mean I could stay in the UK, it also meant keeping regular-ish hours and seeing my dad. Having gone to stage school as a girl, I'd had quite a lot of dance training in the past, but it was a skill I hadn't really used properly for a long while, and I knew it would be great to release my inner hoofer. And frankly, like almost every girl in the country, I loved the costumes.

My God, the costumes! The Chrisanne workshop in Croydon, where some of the *Strictly* outfits are made, was an Aladdin's cave of showbiz delights. I had never seen so many feathers, sequins, rhinestones or so much faux stretch leather. I also had no idea how much work and planning went into creating these handmade couture outfits. Croydon is the spiritual home of ballroom. Derek Hough and his sister, Julianne, from the American version, *Dancing with the Stars*, trained in Croydon. Dancers fly from all over the world to go to Croydon. Croydon is where ballroom's at, and Chrisanne is its shimmering Swarovski-crystal-covered centre.

Among the glitter and the feathers, I met with costume designer Su Judd, with whom I had worked on *The Big Breakfast* years before. Su knew what I liked and knew my body from the olden days, so she was brilliant. Every dress costs a small fortune to make and they are beautiful. The producers don't let you keep them after the show unless you pay full price because Chrisanne sell them on afterwards and the frocks go all over the world: Japan, China, America. It really is an industry with global appeal.

Before turning up, I'd researched lots of images of Marilyn Monroe in *The Prince and the Showgirl* and I had lots of 1950s-inspired ideas. Su and I then worked together to come up with the designs. Naturally I had to have bras sewn into everything because I'm so busty, so we always started with the bra and then built the outfit around it. Support is everything when you're jiggling about. They are hugely unforgiving outfits; every lump, bump, ripple and bulge is on show.

The *Strictly* season kicks off in late summer, when the line-up is announced and you do a photo shoot in your costume. Then the producers announce they're going to pair you with someone, and you have no idea who it will be! There's always a huge amount of speculation about who is going to be put with whom. I was adamant, saying, 'I don't mind who it is just so long as it is not Brendan Cole.'

Brendan was supposed to be the fiery, moody one and he had a reputation for being a bit of a Lothario at the time. A couple of years earlier he had become close to his dance partner Natasha Kaplinsky, which led to rumours in the press. I had been around TV shows long enough to suspect that the producers on *Strictly* would want to focus on the relationships between the professionals and their partners as it gets the public interested and gets them voting. Obviously the relationships aren't usually romantic but you can see on the show that a close bond is formed because you work so closely together. I was very much engaged to Billy and was doing the show because I loved dancing. I didn't really need that extra dynamic of gossip in the media. Needless to say, I should have kept my big mouth shut, because the producers immediately paired me up with Brendan Cole!

In the end, he became a very good friend and a close confidant and was not at all like I'd imagined him to be. To begin with, however, things were tremendously hard. For the first couple of weeks Brendan and I spent every day together and I found the level of intimacy the show demanded very difficult. The dancers are extremely professional, but they do have their hands *all* over you. It is very flirtatious and touchy-feely. I had danced before, but I had never done a live show, so I felt completely out of my comfort zone. I didn't want to put my face next to Brendan's in case Billy was put out, yet a lot of a routine depends on the chemistry you have with your partner, so I tried my best to tread a very fine line. Because of Billy, though, I never really let my guard down with Brendan, and I think our performances suffered as a result.

We started off rehearsing a cha-cha just to see what sort of rhythm I had, and then we went straight into a rhumba, which is the most sexual dance you can do. The rhumba is all about a guy and a girl falling in love and getting sexual. We chose the music and decided to do a *Dirty Dancing* song, and then Brendan choreographed the dance. We got it down in two weeks; the rest of the time was spent polishing and perfecting. The next challenge is obviously trying to work out how you're going to cope with the pressure of nerves, as they can make you forget everything as soon as you walk out onto the floor.

That series of *Strictly* had some fantastic girls: Gabby Logan, Alesha Dixon, Penny Lancaster, Stephanie Beacham and Letitia Dean. There was also Matt Di

Angelo, Gethin Jones, Kenny Logan and Willy Thorne, among others. They were a great gang and we got on well together. When you're on the show, there isn't time to truly learn the dance. Of course you learn your routine and the musicality of a dance like the rhumba, but you don't learn to dance it properly. And once you get your routine down, then all you can try and do is get through it on the night without messing up! If you come from a music or dance background, you can pick it up quite easily. But if you don't, I can see why people struggle. Alesha was brilliant, Gabby was as fit as anything – she could do backbends and the splits – and Penny was a gorgeous leggy blonde. I think Letitia was the one who struggled most with her confidence.

Nobody on *Strictly* knew my dad was extremely ill. Brendan was the only one I told. I kept it like that because it was such a personal thing. It was a really tough time. The car would collect me every morning from my house in Kent and take me to a fitness centre in Chislehurst which had a studio, where I'd meet Brendan, who had come down from London. We'd train all day, and then I'd go back home. Brendan was always incredibly kind and asked me out to things. He'd say, 'There's an event in London tonight. Do you want to come?' There's this; there's that. But all I did was go home, back to Kent, to be with my family.

The *Strictly* producers are a bit optimistic about how

much of your time the show will take up. When you sign up, they tell you that you only really need to do six hours of dancing a day and then the show on Saturday. But in reality you are in the studio from 9 a.m. to 6 p.m. every day, you go on the companion show, *It Takes Two*, during the week, you do endless rounds of publicity, and then there's the main show itself. I have no idea how anyone can do another job at the same time as doing *Strictly*, especially if they want to do well.

Luckily, I loved the show and I loved to dance. It did take up a lot of my time and there were occasions when I had to say, 'I just can't train today. I have to go and see my dad.' I'd just drive down and spend the day with him. Obviously none of the judges knew, so each Saturday when they'd say something like 'Alesha Dixon has trained forty hours this week, but Kelly Brook has only trained for five!' I'd just look lazy. I'd be judged accordingly and they'd come down on me. I felt bad for Brendan, but he was very understanding.

I was completely torn between these two worlds, but at the same time, dancing was the only thing that was getting me through. That and the fact I knew my mum and dad were watching. As a child, my dad used to take me in his truck to dance lessons. The show was something for them to look forward to every Saturday, to watch their little girl on the telly. My dad wasn't going out by then: he was far too ill. In an odd way, I was dancing for myself, but I was really doing it for him. It genuinely made their week. They watched *It Takes Two* every night. It was my therapy and their perfect distraction.

I loved the group dances. They took the pressure off, and the producers brought in different choreographers as well, so they were more fun. The professionals become students again because they are also learning a swing dance or a rock-and-roll number, so we were all slightly more on an equal footing.

There is quite a lot of competition on *Strictly*. The professionals are absolutely fiercely competitive with each other. They want to win, and they want to stay in the competition as long as they can, so they try very hard to get the best out of you. They spend time trying to work out how they can make you appeal to the audience and get the public voting for you. They work miracles sometimes; they even managed to make Ann Widdecombe entertaining!

In *Strictly*, for reasons best known to the press, I garnered most of the media attention and PR, and I remember everyone noticing it. I think maybe it was because I'd been away for a while in LA, or it was the luck of the draw, but I do remember Anton du Beke coming in one Saturday jokingly complaining because he'd been asked what it was like to work with Kelly

Brook – and I wasn't even dancing with him! No one had asked me what it was like to work with Anton.

But the producers definitely get involved in managing the contestants. After one group dance in which I was in the middle, I do recall being moved and replaced by Alesha Dixon. The producer then told me that Matt Di Angelo and I were coming across as too arrogant and all I could think was, You're editing me! But sometimes there are contestants who break through and can really surprise everyone. Kenny Logan couldn't even clap in time to the music, but then he came out in his kilt and started throwing Ola Jordan around and he was completely fabulous. Some people really blossom. There is a moment when you feel like you are a *proper* dancer, your 'Strictly moment', when you feel that you are entertaining the crowd and you've cracked it. It is the moment that makes all the pressure and the long hours worthwhile. It is like disappearing down a spangled K-hole. The first time I was due to perform live, I remember standing backstage and taking these deep breaths, thinking, Why the hell am I putting myself through this? This is an awful existence. Even now I often think that when I am waiting to go on stage. What the hell is all this for?

It was halfway through *Strictly* when Dad suddenly started to look extremely ill and he really deteriorated. My mother called Billy and told him that the cancer had gone to Dad's brain and they'd decided to do radio-therapy on his head. That basically triggered a massive decline.

I remember going down to see him a week before he died and he was chatting away, but he'd lost his hair and looked quite gaunt. He was a shadow of what he was before. I had always said I was going to build another house on my property for him and Mum to live in. I was planning to do up one of the outbuildings, a large oast house, and he was still talking about living there. I think he was keeping his mind active. Making plans. Designing things. Giving them names. He was talking about the future when we both knew there was going to be no future. It made me so sad I snapped at him.

'Dad! Stop talking about the house,' I barked. I felt so guilty, but I couldn't help it.

Now that the cancer had spread to his brain, my dad's behaviour became difficult and unpredictable. He'd suddenly take himself off to see his mother or he'd disappear and we'd find him at my brother's house with his grandkids. My mum wanted to keep an eye on him at all times, but he wouldn't let her. Anything could have happened. He could have had a fit, started bleed-ing; when cancer has gone to the brain, anything is possible. I think my mother's biggest fear was that some-thing was going to happen to my dad when she wasn't there to help him.

When they're filming *Strictly*, they endlessly try to get to shoot some sort of backstory. The producers spend a lot of time trying to get you to go to your grandmother's to have tea; they want you to take the cameras home with you, see your kids, have a chat with your cat, that sort of rubbish. But because my dad was so ill, I always said no. I am not great at that sort of stuff anyway. I only like people to see what I want them to see. And I just couldn't bear the idea of walking into my parents' house and saying, 'Cooee, everyone! Here's my mum. Hi, Mum! And oh look – over here on the sofa is my dad. He's dying. I love you, Dad.' It's not my thing. I have no interest in showing people how 'real' I am on television. I am happy to stand and pose for the cameras, Kelly with the boobs and the big smile, but you ain't coming to Kent!

Little did I know the producers had called my best mate Lisa and organized for a bus to collect everyone from Kent and bring them to the BBC studios! They wanted my family to join in with a surprise samba-themed birthday party in my dressing room. Brendan was in on it and had called Lisa, who had called my mum, but of course no one had called or spoken to me because it was a surprise!

It was terrible. It was a Friday night and we'd finished rehearsing. I was shattered and all I could think about was getting home as quickly as I could to see my family. As I opened the door and walked into my dressing room, they all shouted, 'Surprise!' It was *awful*. I had all these cameras in my face, and I could see my mother, my nan, everyone, but no Dad. I wanted to throw up. I had managed to keep the cameras away from everyone all this time and now suddenly this. My family came because they thought I wanted them to be there. It could not have been further from the truth. The camera panned towards my mum as the producer said, 'This week, Kelly is going to dance to "Saturday Night Fever". She says that was the first date you and your husband went on?'

My mum and my aunt just looked at each other and started to sob. I was so mortified; all I could do was laugh like an idiot. I'd chosen that song as a special message to my parents, a private message. I'd imagined Mum and Dad finding out together when they watched the show at home. Instead, Mum's reaction was being filmed. It was awful, awful, awful. We were all laughing and crying at the same time. I tried to pretend it was fun and I danced a samba for the camera, smiling and saying, 'Look! My family is here!' and all the time wishing the cameras would just go away and thinking, Dad must be really ill if he hasn't come to this. He must be really weak if he can't make it from the sofa to the car. I must get home. I've got to get home. I have to get home. Three days later, he died.

It was Brendan who told me my father was dying. I was about to do *It Takes Two* with Claudia Winkleman when my mum called him. She thought it would be easier for him to tell me than for her. I am not sure she could have got the words out. He came up to me and said, 'Kelly, you've got to go home. Now.' I could tell by the look on his face that it was serious and it was time.

I drove to my parents' house as quickly as I could, but I could feel Dad slipping away. I said goodbye to him as I was driving. I said, 'Dad, if you want to go now, then go.' By the time I arrived, he had already gone. My brother was there, holding his hand, and Dad just looked peaceful, like he was sleeping. His death was very dignified in the end. They had put him on a morphine drip and he'd slowly slipped into a coma and then passed away.

2

From Here to Italia Conti

Every weekend it would go off in my house. My mum was very young when she got married and had kids, and my dad really did like a drink. It caused a lot of trouble when I was growing up. I don't want to label him an alcoholic, because he wasn't, but drinking did make him aggressive. There were countless fights and I think my mum got so used to the dynamic that if there wasn't any tension, then she would almost make it happen.

We lived in a second-floor flat in Stirling Close, an unremarkable council estate in Borstal, a suburb of Rochester, famous only for its juvenile prison. My earliest memory was of my mother throwing an iron down the stairwell at my dad after he came back late from the pub.

I used to dread the weekend. Sundays especially. Sunday was pub day. We used to have a roast dinner every Sunday, and every other Sunday it would be burned. My parents would spend too long in the pub, come home pissed and eat the burned Sunday lunch; then there'd be a fight and the police would be called. Or my dad would drive off in his truck. He'd drive to the end of the road and fall asleep in the cab. I'd walk down the road and knock on the door.

'Dad, Dad, are you going to come home?'

He'd just grunt and go back to sleep. It was somehow more embarrassing when he drove off after a fight, as the neighbours recognized my dad's truck parked on the street, and of course they'd see my dad fast asleep, pickled up in the front. Damian and I were usually tucked up in bed by the time he made it home and the next morning we'd be back to normal. Until it happened again.

One of the worst times was when my dad came back from the pub and started throwing furniture around, while Mum and I huddled out of the way. My mother called the police and my dad tried to climb out of the window to escape. My dad broke his leg trying to avoid them and they had to carry him down the stairs. It was one of the most traumatic events in my childhood. I will never forget it. They took him to the cells and when I went to see him in hospital two days later, his face was black and blue from the escape attempt. It was shocking. I was thirteen.

I wasn't born in Stirling Close. I was actually born

in a bedsit on 23 November 1979 a little bit further down the road. Not literally, obviously – I was born in Chatham Hospital. My mum was seventeen, and Dad was twenty-nine.

My mum, Sandra Kelly, had a best friend called Lesley Parsons and they always played together. Also born and brought up in Rochester, Lesley had three brothers. One, Kenneth, was a bit older and Mum always had a crush on him. Initially, Kenneth went off, married and had a daughter, Sasha, but he and his wife separated and eventually got divorced. Sandra knew Sasha very well, as she was always at her friend Lesley's house, and then after the divorce, Ken went travelling to Sardinia and when he returned, he suddenly noticed that Sandra had 'grown up'. They quickly fell in love and were married at Chatham Register Office. They were like childhood sweethearts, and I think, despite the rows and the fighting, my parents remained so right up until the point that my father died. I actually remember her being furious after my dad had gone.

'We went through all the rubbish,' she said, 'the drama, the fights, all that shit, and when it finally gets good, he dies.' She couldn't believe it. He'd eventually calmed down and then he was gone.

The baby of her family, my mum was gorgeous, pretty and blonde with a petite, tiny figure. But she was also a powerhouse. She was the one who secured us a council flat and eventually, when I was about five, a council house where she still lives today. She had grown up on the rough Davis Estate in Rochester. Her father was in the army, but eventually he became a builder, and her mother, Ann Kelly, was a rather glamorous woman who didn't work. I always remember her in fur coats, smoking cigarettes and sipping gin and tonics. My nan was just seventeen when she married, and went on to have three kids. My mother had an elder sister, Patricia, otherwise known as Patsy, who became a journalist, ultimately moving to Belgium and working for CNN. She headed up their bureau in Brussels, running their European office when they launched. She and my mother chose very different paths.

My mother also had a younger brother, called David, who tragically was killed at the age of sixteen. He was run over by a car. My mother called me Kelly to keep the family name alive for another generation. Both she and her sister were keen to call their sons David after their brother, but Patsy got there first. She has two children, my cousins Sally and David. So my mother called my little brother, who came along just over a year and a half after me, Damian.

As I said earlier, my dad was a scaffolder, but he had a slightly more colourful past than my mother. He worked on building sites, but at the same time anything he could get away with he did. When he was younger he'd been on remand for robbery. He was the getaway driver for a group of would-be thieves, and they all got caught. In fact, growing up, the only time you ever saw my dad in a suit, he was going to court! It was just for minor things, though, usually related to drinking too much.

My childhood was a lot more bucolic than it sounds. It's true Rochester bled into Chatham, which bled into Gillingham, making up the urban spread of the Medway towns. And granted, the flat I grew up in was grotty, on the top of a steep hill, buffeted by the stiff breeze that came off the river Medway, with glorious views of the M2 motorway; but it was right on the edge of the countryside. We were minutes away from poppy fields and long grass. Damian and I were not only close in age but we were very close as siblings as well. We'd play schools together (he was always my pupil), and I was very protective of him. I adored him; he was such a cute little brother. We'd spend hours climbing trees, building camps, looking for slow-worms. We weren't urban kids at all; we were not on street corners; we were very out-doorsy.

Dance was my thing. Damian was very boyish, obsessed with knives and guns. He watched all those 1980s movies like *Rambo*, *Predator* and *Kickboxer* – anything with Stallone or Schwarzenegger – while I was very girlie indeed. My obsession was with the TV show *Fame*.

I think that programme in particular was a huge influence on a whole generation of girls like me, Emma Bunton and Victoria Beckham. It was set at the New York High School for Performing Arts, with kids dancing on tables; they were kids with a dream, aspirations to get out of where they were from. They wanted to make it in the big city. I related to it hugely. And I loved dancing. I have a scar on my eyebrow where my face had to be butterfly-stitched after I leaped off the sofa doing a *Fame* jump while pretending to be Leroy. I lived and breathed it. I loved classical ballet, but I was even more into jazz and modern dance. I was desperate to be a dancer and choreographer.

My half-sister, Sasha, was a huge influence on me. Ten years my senior, she had gone to live with her maternal grandmother after her mother died in a car accident. Her grandmother was quite wealthy and had sent Sasha to the Italia Conti Academy of Theatre Arts, which she'd hated. But it opened doors for her and Sasha went on to become a big fashion model. She worked for *Vogue* and *Playboy*; she travelled the world. We used to love it when Sasha came to stay when we were kids. We'd all get excited and jump around, saying, 'Sasha's coming! Sasha's here!' She would always have the coolest stuff and the best haircuts. She was the first person I saw who'd had their belly button pierced. She was out there doing everything, travelling, going to

33

Australia, living the dream. She was enough to put stars into any little girl's eyes.

Meanwhile, my life revolved round the local pub, the David Copperfield. As kids, we would be in there, sitting in the smoke, keeping out of the way under the table with a glass of Coke and a packet of pork scratchings. From a very young age I would see fistfights, shouting matches. I'd hear terrible language and see so much violence. Damian and I would see and hear everything. It was awful having to look after him, as he was much more sensitive than I was.

But it was our social life too. We'd meet up with other kids from the pub; we'd go on coach trips to the races and to Thorpe Park. There was a period when the pub was run by a really lovely couple who were much more family-orientated and as a result the people who went there were too. But when the landlords changed, so did the customers.

I remember one bloke having his head repeatedly smashed against the bar and his nose exploding and blood pouring everywhere. It was disgusting. It was so violent and horrific. It is no wonder I now don't want any drama in my life. I don't understand people who do drugs; I don't understand why people want volatile relationships.

Not that my early years were all bad, obviously. It's true that my parents weren't well off. I do remember hiding behind the sofa and turning off the lights when anyone knocked at the door asking for money or to see the TV licence. But there was enough money to get by; my dad might have liked a drink, but he was a conscientious, proud man who never missed a day's work. And everyone always made an effort at Christmas.

My nan would arrive on Christmas Eve to stay for a couple of days and she would insist on us playing lots of games, like wrapping yourself up in a hat, scarf and gloves and trying to eat a bar of chocolate with a knife and fork. We'd play card games and charades, and she would also always insist on us opening a present before Christmas Day, because she couldn't wait. My mother would be screaming, 'No!' and Nan would be urging us on. But eventually Nan would win and we would get to open a present on Christmas Eve.

I remember one year finding out where my mother had put all the presents and climbing up into the cupboard and pulling them all down, unwrapping them and wrapping them back up again. The disappointment the next day was terrible. It was probably the worst Christmas of my life. I wasn't even that young to be so naughty! I was nine!

The David Copperfield used to have disco nights every Friday with a DJ *and* lights! That's when I fell in love with music and dancing. My parents would have a few beers and I'd be on the Coke and pork scratchings, dancing for hours to Kim Wilde's 'Rockin' Around the Christmas Tree', surrounded by fag smoke.

I can't imagine taking children into that sort of environment now, but that was the culture of the time. Things were very different in those days. People's choices were very limited; there weren't many options. My family never ate in restaurants, for example. Never, ever. Our treat would be having a McDonald's every Thursday. We'd go into town and shop at the Saver Centre and then have a cheeseburger, chips and a Coke on the way home. But that would be it.

My mum was always quite fun. I can picture her in the kitchen gossiping with her friends, mug of tea in one hand, cigarette in the other. She was gregarious and liked having a good time. She wasn't the kind of mum who got up in the morning and made us breakfast. Damian and I were both pretty independent: we'd get ourselves up and make our own breakfasts, and we'd always walk ourselves to school. She wasn't one of those smothering mums. She just did her own thing, and we did our own thing. Sometimes that's a good thing, as it teaches you to become self-sufficient from an early age. I remember once not getting up for school and my mother going completely mad! She dragged me out of bed and made damn sure I went to school. There was no slacking in our house!

I'd finish school at 3 p.m., come home and Mum

would have laid out sandwiches and cakes, as she wouldn't be home until about 5 p.m. I was a bit of a latchkey kid. But with both parents working, there were not that many options around. Dad was out scaffolding, and Mum had various part-time jobs. When I was older, my mum worked part-time in the local frozen-food factory. She was employed by Tiffany Sharwood's in research and development, working with the scientists to come up with recipes. I think she really enjoyed that time and she was always coming home with frozen food and mango chutneys. We lived on the stuff.

I went to Delce Junior School and was one of the brightest in my class. I think if I had bothered to think about the eleven-plus, or indeed engaged my brain, I might well have passed it. But it was the first exam I had ever taken, I had zero preparation, and I didn't really know what I was doing. It was multiple choice, and I remember sitting there while my brain was completely elsewhere. My best friend at the time, Louise, passed and she went to Chatham Grammar School for Girls, while I went to Thomas Aveling, a large, modern comprehensive that was about half an hour's walk down the road. Louise was a very good influence on me. Her parents worked at the garden centre and were a nice family. I liked going to play at her house because they were calm, kind and polite. I really wanted to follow her. I was going to appeal against my eleven-plus result, but in the end I had other plans and dreams. I was determined to go to stage school come what may. So what did I care if I spent some time at Thomas Aveling, the same school my mother went to?

It was quite a rough school; there were fights and pupils who got expelled. There were thirty-two in a class, so it was quite easy to disappear or indeed bunk off, which, I have to say, I did not. I didn't smoke or drink. I was a bit of a show-off at school, a bit rebellious, the sort of kid who sits at the back of the class, but I never puffed away behind the bike sheds – that wasn't my style. I didn't hate it there, but there were not many extra-curricular activities. It was work or sport; there was no drama or dance, nothing there for me. Instead, I went dancing two nights a week at the local dance academies, Kicks, Elaine's Stage School and Dance House.

Ballet was my escapism; it was the only thing that made me truly happy. I could see my friends at school already getting into trouble. I had one mate who'd started to shoplift. She asked me to come with her once so we headed for the shopping centre in Chatham. I remember we went to Top Shop, pinched a top and got caught. I had money – I'd just had my birthday – so I could have paid for the top, but that wasn't the point. That was what was going on around me, this was the culture, so I just did it. I think it was out of boredom. I'd bought some trousers and my mate wanted a top, so she pinched it and then lost her bottle and told me to take it out of the shop.

The security guards followed us onto the bus, where we tried to hide, but they marched us off by the scruffs of our necks. It was a very-public humiliation. My friend was crying hysterically in the police station.

'Relax, we're not going to prison,' I said – a bit too cockily as it turned out.

'Yes, you are,' one of the policemen said. 'With that attitude, you're heading towards a young offenders' institute.'

To teach me a lesson, he popped me in a cell. I remember sitting there reading all the graffiti and feeling very sorry for myself. My friend, still sobbing gently, got a can of Coke and a reassuring smile.

Meanwhile, the police turned up at our house, only to find that my parents weren't home. It was the weekend, so naturally they were in the pub. When they got my mother out of the pub, she wasn't worried about me; she was only worried about what my dad might have had stashed away. After she'd come to the police station and sprung us, she kept saying, 'You idiot, Kelly. Your dad could have had anything in the garage. You gave me a heart attack.'

Later, when my friend and I turned up at the pub, all the blokes at the bar started to shout, 'Hide your wallets, lads!' Like we were a couple of Fagin's kids. They thought it was a massive joke. In fact there was a trend at the time for kids to nick things and then bring them into school to show off to their mates. God knows what would have happened to me if I had stayed in Rochester.

I was quite a pretty teenager, so I used to get invited out a lot, but the other girls at school didn't like it, so I was picked on. It was quite full on. It was fight or flight and you constantly had to be on your guard, looking out for trouble. There was always someone who wanted to fight me. I looked old for my age. I would hitch up my skirt and wear my tie crookedly. And I had a perm and scrunchy hair. I'd get through a can of hairspray a week. I had the proper chav look. At the time, the more jewellery you wore, the better. My mum would always buy me gold for Christmas and birthdays. I'd wear gold hooped earrings and gold rings on every finger. I had the full collection: sovereign rings, keeper rings, gate brace-lets, belcher chains, Krugerrands. It was like armour. If you looked like a tough girl, they'd leave you alone a little more. I vividly remember sitting on the sofa going through the Argos catalogue and picking out the rings I wanted. I was a proper Chatham girl.

In the first year of secondary, I had a boyfriend. He was a third year, Steve, and lived above the David Cop-perfield. He had huge afro hair, blue eyes and braces (as did I) and spots (as did I), and I fell in love with him at first sight. We had a kiss in the woods. I went out with him for nine months.

It was all very innocent and sweet. We'd go up to my tiny little box bedroom, with its single bed and pink wallpaper with a chintzy border, and kiss. I didn't have any posters on the wall, I don't think. All I really remember is my hairdryer and a massive can of hairspray. My perm was important to me! Perms were very important!

The local youth centre was run by my friend Leah's mother, Lesley, in the youth wing at school. We'd go home, change, have tea and come back to school to hang out in the youth wing and play pool, eat ice lollies and graffiti the building; it was the usual stuff. Lesley was brilliant. I remember her organizing a trip to Amsterdam. We went on the ferry!

As this was the 1990s, a lot of the boys were beginning to smoke and go to raves, but I didn't. All I did was buy sweets; I was so square. I had so many other interests, like theatre and performing. My mum used to call me Saffy, after the character in *Ab Fab* – that's how square I was. My mum and her mate would be smoking and drinking in the kitchen and I'd come down, find them and be utterly disgusted!

Steve left Thomas Aveling which was very inconvenient for our budding romance because of course he wasn't around during the school day any more. I do, however, recall him coming back to school one day while I was in a science class. I heard him hissing at the window, trying to get my attention. He and his mate

41

said they were going to sneak into the classroom. They snuck through a window and crept in the back, which they were, of course, not allowed to do. They sat next to me and did the experiments and it was a while before the teacher noticed they were there. She started shouting and yelling and they got up and ran away. I thought he was so cool for doing that! It was proper love. He gave me a gold ring from the Argos catalogue with hearts all over it. I've still got it! It's in my memory box.

I was a dreamer. I have always been a dreamer. My dreams kept me sane when things were rough and tough, which they often were, and my dreams kept me going. There was nothing for me in Kent, and Rochester is not the sort of place dreams are made of or somewhere they are likely to come true. All I ever wanted was to get out, go to London and to stage school. Aged thirteen, by sheer force of will, I did just that.

It must have been my half-sister who put the idea of going to stage school in my head or maybe it was just that I was at dance school and that's all we talked about – Italia Conti, Sylvia Young; Sylvia Young, Italia Conti. I wanted to do musical theatre. I wanted to be a backing dancer in pop videos. I wanted to be on TV, in films. My mum wanted me to be Catherine Zeta-Jones in *The Darling Buds of May*. She used to say, 'You'd be good in that, Kelly,' and, 'You should have done that, Kelly.' A lot of my mates at the time didn't have any interests or ambitions; they had no idea what they wanted. I was very motivated, and most importantly, my mum believed in me and believed I could do it. She was very supportive and ambitious for me. I am not sure if she *actually* believed I could do it or if she was just pleased and relieved I had an interest. Either way, she never ceased to encourage me, and she took me to the Italia Conti Academy of Theatre Arts for an audition.

I remember the audition very well. Mum and I went on the train. It was only the second time in my life I had been to London. My dad had taken me to Madame Tussauds before, but that had been it. London was only thirty miles away but could have been the other side of the world.

My ballet school had helped me prepare for the audition. I'd had extra lessons every Saturday for the past six weeks. I had to prepare a tap, ballet and jazz dance number as well as two acting set pieces and a song. I remember singing 'Especially for You' almost as soulfully as Kylie Minogue and Jason Donovan and doing a set piece from *Antigone*. The pressure I put myself under was immense, but I really did give it my best shot, which, I suppose, was all I could hope to do. The wait was only a week long, but it felt like an eternity. When the envelope finally arrived, I ripped it opened and probably screamed the house down with joy! I was in! I'd got a place!

But there was a problem. My parents couldn't afford to send me. Rochester Council wouldn't give me a grant – weirdly, loads of Essex girls went to Italia Conti, because that council had a grant system for dancers that paid the fees, but Rochester didn't. There was nothing we could do. I had got a place, but I couldn't go. Then suddenly, out of the blue, my great-uncle Michael, my nan's brother, who lived in South Africa, very generously offered to pay for the first two terms. I couldn't believe it. It was so incredibly kind of him; I owe him a lot.

Thereafter the school, when they'd seen how dedicated and hardworking I was, offered me a scholarship to continue studying there. So I didn't have to pay. They had a scheme whereby you could pay the school back any fees owing by taking on commercial work. So whatever money I earned through the school's talent agency would be kept back and would go towards paying my school fees. That's the way it was. I didn't have much choice. I learned from a very early age how to sing for my supper.

Italia Conti, which is on Goswell Road, near the Barbican, was very different from Thomas Aveling. For a start, the uniform came from Harrods. My mum complained vociferously.

'What the hell is the matter with Marks and Spencer? Only you, Kelly,' she said, 'would have a school uniform that comes from bloody Harrods.'

It was a two-hour train journey to get to the Knights-bridge department store, and when she saw the price of the clothes, my mum insisted on getting everything about three sizes too big so that I would *never* grow out of them. We bought a light blue kilt, a white cotton shirt and a dark blue blazer.

The night before I turned up to school, my mum decided to attack my mono-brow. She pinned me down on the bed, numbed my skin with ice cubes and plucked my eyebrows into slim, high arches. It was agony. I screamed and laughed hysterically as my mum wielded the tweezers. The next day, my first day at school, I arrived with a slightly surprised look on my face and a kilt that – in spite of my mum's best efforts – was at least three inches too short. Everyone else's nearly reached the floor, while mine was to the knee. I had already got something wrong. But it was the eyebrows that fascin-ated everyone else. Within two or three days of arriving most of the girls in my class had copied my plucked look, some more successfully and less drastically than others.

The daily commute to London was hard for someone of my age. I left home at 6.30 a.m. to catch the 7 a.m. train. My mum would drop me off, give me my £1.50 dinner money and hand me over to another Italia Conti student, Natasha Green, who lived two stops further down the same train line. Natasha would lean out of the window, grab me and we'd travel in together, ready for a nine-o'-clock start. Some days I'd leave home even earlier so that I could go for a swim at the Barbican pool before class.

The average school day was full on. The day would start with a 9 a.m. ballet class, followed by an hour of tap, then an acting class, then lunch, then singing and then academic studies. We'd finish at 5.30 p.m. and then I'd get back on the train to Rochester. It was like a double school day. It was not like we were replacing maths with dancing; we were doing maths *and* dancing. I'd be home by 7 p.m., when I'd have dinner and then do my homework. It was a long day for a thirteen-year-old.

I was never the star pupil. To be honest, I wasn't a great singer, and it was a musical theatre school, so that held me back a lot. There were some girls who could really belt out a tune to Elaine Paige standard, but I was a chorus girl. I could hold a tune and kick my legs high and smile. I was all tits and teeth. It was always about the performance. Even at the local dance schools I went to, I was never the best dancer, but I would always get the award for the best performance. I would put on the best show. I would be put in the middle and at the front, and I'd sell it. I'd sell it hard.

I grew boobs quite early on, when I was twelve or thirteen, and was quite a sexy little girl, which was not an advantage. Casting directors used to come to Conti to look for children for TV shows and commercials, and I looked much older than I actually was, which was the opposite of what they wanted! They wanted girls who looked young for their age. A twelve-year-old who could play an eight-year-old was much more likely to get work than a thirteen-year-old with a double-D chest who looked the right side of legal. In my first headshots, photographed using a wind machine, I had the plucked eyebrows and was wearing a white shirt. My mum had made me have braces when I was ten years old, so I'd had that train-tracks thing going on. By the time I was thirteen, I had the full Hollywood smile, the eyebrows and a rather large bust. It looked totally wrong! The school cropped my boobs out of the shot in the hope that I didn't look quite so old but there was no hiding my shape when I got to the auditions. I did get small parts on the odd television show and I did panto, but no major roles.

The other girls didn't like me very much, especially the older ones in Natasha Green's class. Natasha herself was lovely, but the others were quite spiteful. I think because I had big boobs, looked older and the boys noticed me, some of the older girls were a bit jealous. I had never really experienced psychological bullying before and it was the first time I had been properly targeted. It was all rather difficult. At least in comprehensive when someone didn't like you, they just came up, swore at you and punched you in the face and you knew where you were. But drama-school girls were all kissy-kissy and much more manipulative, gossipy and clever about spreading rumours. It was nasty. I would have much preferred to have got it over and done with, with a quick fight, a smack in the face, but they just made you feel horrible and not want to be there. I had never experienced anything like it before.

At stage school, you are being groomed to be a professional artist of some sort, whereas a comprehensive is all about getting as many GCSEs as possible so you can stay on and do your A levels. There is a lot more pressure at stage school, and because the classes are so much smaller, it is harder to make friends, as there are fewer people to choose from. Also, everyone comes from very different backgrounds. At a local school, you probably know the brother or sister of the pupils in your class already, and all your parents know each other. It is a community. But getting on a train to commute two hours to school means you're not going to know anyone. There were students from Sheffield, from abroad and plenty of posh rich kids. I had much more in common with the kids at Thomas Aveling than I did with those at Italia Conti.

I remember thinking the girls in my class were like babies. They were little girls and quite immature. None of them had kissed a boy, whereas I had. I was already well on the way through puberty. I had the big boobs and the plucked eyebrows, and was much more street-wise than any of them.

The only other person like me was Dannielle Brent, who has gone on to have a great career as an actress, starring in *Bad Girls*. There was a ridiculous rumour that she'd given a boy a blowjob, which of course she hadn't, but I knew immediately she would be my best friend. We bonded because we were two slags together. We weren't, but for a while that's what everyone seemed to think!

Weight was also a big issue at the school. It was very competitive, and girls were in a leotard and tights all the time, so there was obvious pressure to conform and be slim. There were endless chats about what diets were good and what everyone was eating. I had one friend who was bulimic, but she was also a feeder. I felt extremely sorry for her and by way of compensation I used to match her slice of cake for slice of cake. The only thing was, she'd vomit it all up again, whereas I would squirrel it gently away on my thighs! I remember my ballet teacher telling me off for putting on weight, and also my mum calling me the 'Sugar Plum Fairy' as I had put on half a stone.

The school was busy all the time and there was always something going on. There was a casting agency on the top floor, with a board outside where all the auditions and castings were posted, which everyone would check every day. Also, we would each get notes left on the noticeboard downstairs saying, 'Kelly to the agency', telling you to check upstairs. They were constantly submitting our headshots and CVs to casting directors in the hope of us getting jobs. I was always up for *East-Enders* parts and bits in *Grange Hill* because of my accent. Anything cockney, dodgy or a little bit rough, I'd be put up for it. Whereas my friend Catherine, who had a beautiful received pronunciation accent, was always at the RSC doing Shakespeare with Jude Law. It used to drive me mad. I know I'm common, but I could easily have done a posh voice if given the chance.

At the end of every term, we did a show at the Avondale Theatre, which was a bit like the Royal Variety. There was always a lot of buzz and excitement about who was going to get such and such a part and who was taking the leads. Occasionally agents would come down and have a look to see if there was anyone they wanted to put on their books. Italia Conti was one of the first ports of call for anyone looking for young musical talent. When Michael Jackson was in town for the Brit Awards, in 1996, they came and cast a whole load of kids to dance with him on stage when he performed 'Earth Song'. I remember a girl called Vicky who had the most fabulous voice and went on to sing with Michael, while Jarvis Cocker flapped his bum at the audience.

I earned a bit of money by getting a Saturday job when I was fourteen or fifteen. The city of Rochester is full of tea shops, antique shops and OAPs. The cathedral and the surrounding area are beautiful. There are cobbled streets, and it is home to the second oldest school in the world, King's Rochester, founded in 604. Charles Dickens wrote some of his novels in Rochester and every year there is the Dickens Festival, when everyone dresses up as famous characters from his books. It is a pretty city, and the High Street is charming.

Sadly, my parents lived a long way from the High Street. Not that that deterred me from walking the hour and a half there and back every Saturday when I worked at the Precinct Pantry, a gorgeous little tea room right next door to the cathedral. I think I was determined to have a little bit of glamour even then, and the most glamorous thing around was the Precinct Pantry. The three-hour round trip was not going to put me off. The cakes were delicious, the crockery was pretty and dainty, and the boarding-school boys from King's were a little bit flirtatious. I didn't earn very much money, and obviously I had to walk miles, but I think it was the elegant fantasy that kept me going.

During the holidays I'd either be working at the Precinct Pantry or occasionally dancing in pantomime or cabaret shows for a company called Hammond Productions – it was more fun and entertaining than it was lucrative. Or if Damian and I were lucky, we'd go to Brussels.

I used to love staying with my aunt Patsy in Belgium. She always lived in beautiful country houses, and she always had interesting people over for dinner. She had dinner parties! She was intelligent and interested in politics. Her life felt a world away from Rochester, but she loved having her little sister's kids over for the holidays and would spoil us rotten.

When she was working as the senior international correspondent for CNN, she lived in a gorgeous farmhouse just outside Brussels with flocks of chickens and geese. Sometimes we'd go over for Christmas, but it was mainly Easter, and she would organize these massive egg hunts and hide delicious Belgian chocolates all over the farm. It would keep us busy for hours!

Patsy was a huge influence on me. She was a great inspiration. She was always flying here, there and everywhere interviewing amazing people. I remember watching her in a flak jacket reporting from Kosovo, Sarajevo or Russia and being so impressed. She was freelance for a lot of the time and then worked for CNN for many years. She was so smart and very strong and passionate about journalism, and never aligned herself with any particular party or newspaper. I remember her taking me in to the CNN studios in Brussels when I was about twelve. I found the whole thing so exciting, if a little bit overwhelming.

My uncle Nigel, Patsy's husband, was a musician and an artist. My cousins Sally and David had an idyllic, truly creative childhood that was really quite privileged. They learned classical piano, spoke fluent French and both went to university, where Sally studied politics and David studied law. They were, and are, properly educated, cultured, grounded and nice. Perfect children. It is extraordinary that two sisters can end up taking such different paths in life.

Even now Sally says how lucky she was, and it shows in the careers she and her brother have managed to forge for themselves. David works as a contractual lawyer in New York, and Sally makes TV documentaries. I see Sally nearly every day when I am in the UK; she is like my best friend. But when we were growing up, she idolized me! I was like the edgy cool kid from the council estate. I'd arrive wearing lipstick and say things like 'Sally, can I crimp your hair?', 'Sally, can I pluck your eyebrows?', 'Sally, can I curl your lashes?' She was never allowed to wear make-up and was always dressed in pretty flowery dresses; her mother was extremely protective of her. Whereas Damian and I were given free rein. We were like little street rats. We'd make Sally listen to

Madonna, dress her up in black lace tights and teach her dance routines. She, of course, loved it!

★

When I was sixteen, my parents said I had to leave Italia Conti at the end of the school year. My mum turned round and said, 'I don't know what more they could teach you. It's time you got a job.'

It was devastating. I didn't know what to do. It was like the door to a new world had been opened and then firmly shut in my face.

But I had no choice. Although I had auditioned for another scholarship which would take me through to eighteen – and I did get it – it covered my tuition fees but not anything else. Money was tight in my house and my parents had been making immense sacrifices for years to send me to that school. Just the train fare and the £1.50-a-day dinner money were enough to make them feel the pinch. I had to get a job.

My two best friends, Dannielle Brent and Natasha Symms, did stay on. They passed their A levels and then both got parts in *Hollyoaks* within six months of leaving Conti. They moved to Liverpool and started working on the show, and although it was not Emmy award-winning, they were on set, working and learning. And that's what you want to do. Work and learn. It was so depressing that I wouldn't have that chance. There were others, like my friend Danny Mays, who is now the lead in all the Mike Leigh films, who went on to RADA. But I couldn't. It still upsets me now, thinking about it, and at the time I was devastated. I was desperate to go to RADA. I was talented enough, just as talented as all the others. Acting is one of those skills you only really start to develop as an artist and performer when you're seventeen or eighteen, when you become an adult and your emotional range is much more sophisticated. But my training stopped when I was sixteen. I was still a kid.

I have often wondered what my life would have been like if I could have taken some fantasy path and gone to the City of London School for Girls, to university and then on to RADA, but those options weren't available to a girl like me. My family could never have afforded university. It was never even spoken about in the house; it simply wasn't an option for us. My brother joined the army at sixteen. Fortunately, he did want to join up, but there aren't that many careers open to young teenagers with a few GCSEs who aren't allowed to stay on at school even if they want to.

Being at Italia Conti for those four years was a gift. I came away with nine GCSEs (which is not bad considering it was a performing arts school) and a bag load of confidence. Although there were times when I was bullied and told off, ultimately it set me up for what I do now. I don't regret going there. I hung out in London and met lots of different people from lots of different backgrounds. It made me realize there was a big world out there, far bigger than Rochester and Kent.

I know now that you miss out on so much if you don't have a great education. Sadly, I didn't. I would love to have had one. I have done the best with what I've had and that is all one can hope for in life. And my parents did the best they could, given the cards they had been dealt and the choices they made. I would have loved to have done A levels, but I did what I did because I had no other choice. It was that simple.

When I left school aged sixteen, it was time for me to make my own choices and start being responsible for who I wanted to be and where I wanted to go. I was determined never to let myself be a product of my environment, my education or the limited expectations of others.

As for what happened next – given where I came from, it was the only move I could make. I don't know what else I could have done.

3

Becoming Kelly Brook

When I approached the door of the Samantha Bond modelling agency in spring 1996, I was sixteen years old and dressed in my Italia Conti school uniform.

To be honest, it was not where I wanted, or expected, to be, but needs must, as they say, and I knew I'd be leaving school in a few months. I needed to earn a living. As my parents had explained, there was no such thing as a free ride and I had to start paying my way.

It was a Friday evening, around six o'clock and dark outside, and Samantha Bond was about to close. This was my last-chance saloon. I had completely run out of options. For the past couple of months or so I'd been to every single modelling agency in London. In those days, the agencies would have open afternoons where young girls, hopefuls, could turn up, be snapped with a Polaroid camera and assessed for their supermodel potential. All desperate to be the new Kate Moss, or Eva Herzigova, we'd sit there waiting to be called by some skinny booker inevitably dressed in black. Then we'd walk up and down reception, while every inch of us was scrutinized, before being swiftly ejected back onto the street.

I'd started out at Models 1, where my elder sister, Sasha, was signed. She had been hugely successful fronting some large advertising campaigns, including Marks & Spencer, and had earned a small fortune along the way. But within a few seconds of my being there it was fairly obvious I was not the right height or shape for them. I was 5 foot 6 inches with a 30E chest, 24-inch waist and 36-inch hips. I was far too short with massive boobs and a curvy body; I had completely the wrong proportions. I was a round, sexy girl when the whole heroin-chic waif thing was at its height. I really was on a hiding to nothing. I remember them being kind and giving me a long list of all the other modelling agents in London to try, and right at the bottom of the list, past Elite, Storm, Premier and Select, were Yvonne Paul and Samantha Bond.

So as I'd been rejected, over a period of two months, by every other agency on the list, here I was, about to meet Samantha Bond – agent to glamour girls, Page Three girls, give-out girls and all those sexy girls you see in pop videos.

As I walked down a dark alley to find the door, my heart sank. Right next door to a pub on the King's Road, it certainly didn't look glamorous like the other agencies. In fact, it was about as far away from 'supermodel' as you could be. And I was clearly never going to be one of those. I remembered seeing the Eva Herzigova 'Hello, boys' Wonderbra campaign and thinking, Wouldn't that be fantastic, to be on a giant billboard? I was so very disappointed to end up here, down an alley next to a pub, rejected by the fashion world I had hankered after. But I was out of options.

In my heart of hearts, although I wanted to be a fashion model, I thought this was probably where I should be. I wasn't tall or thin. I looked like these girls. I was the same as them. Why was I desperate to be something that I was not?

Apart from the model agencies, I had also written to most of the capital's acting agents: William Morris, ICM, Peters, Fraser & Dunlop . . . Needless to say, they had all turned me down, as Italia Conti trained you to be more of a West End Wendy than a serious Shakespearean thesp clutching a skull and wondering where Yorick went. I'd sent out more headshots and CVs than you could shake a stick at. All of it had been hopeless.

The door to the agency was hard to open, and when I finally stumbled in, Samantha Bond was peering at me over her glasses from behind a large leather-topped desk. She was an older lady with bleached-blonde hair, not what I was expecting at all. Alongside her was her colleague, Paul, who was in his mid-thirties with shoulder-length curly brown hair. And that was it. Just the two of them. The rest of the office was a tip. It was covered with paper, piles of invoices, letters, contact sheets. Photos were pinned to a large noticeboard; it was more like a shambolic, dusty detective agency than anything you'd associate with the wonderful world of glamour.

'Hello. I'm Kelly,' I said.

'Hello, Kelly,' replied Sam with her posh Aussie twang, swiftly looking me up and down. 'Do you want a cup of tea?'

After about ten minutes of chat plus a Bourbon biscuit, she said, 'You're very pretty. I like your look. We could do something with you. Yes. We'd like to sign you and do a test shoot. When are you free?'

It took me a while to understand exactly what she'd said. I couldn't believe it. After all this time, suddenly someone had said yes. She said she wanted to send me to a photographer to do some pictures and see how I got on. I was over the moon I'd finally got an agent. I did have one reservation, though. The biggest girl they had on their books at the time was Joanne Guest, who did *Loaded*, Page Three, *Hustler* and *Penthouse*, and that was very far away from what I wanted to do. So I said to Sam that I was sixteen, still at school, wanted to be an actress and didn't want to take my clothes off or do Page Three.

She was charming, and both she and Paul took it in their stride; they didn't bat an eyelid. I signed on the metaphorical dotted line and I remember grinning like the cat that got the cream the entire trip back to Rochester on the train. I was on my way. At last. I had a shot at the big time and I had something lined up, something to do after I had done my GCSEs and left school.

A few days later, the agency organized a shoot with a photographer who did simple black-and-white shots in lingerie and some dresses to put towards a portfolio. I was nervous, but I wasn't a complete novice in the world of modelling.

For years my mum had been entering me into every single competition on the back of a crisp packet, fag packet, any packet she could find. Miss Pears, the Bisto kids, Miss Crazy Paving 1983 . . . anything and everything, she'd fill in the form and send off a photo of me. I am not sure what possessed her to do it, whether she genuinely thought I was the most beautiful child ever to have walked the earth, which, judging by the photos, I very obviously was not, or whether she was simply ambitious for me. And my nan was just as bad. She was always pulling out coupons from crap magazines or cutting off the backs of boxes of Daz and sending away terrible photos of me, with braces and bunches, in the hope that I'd win something.

Occasionally it worked. I was crowned 'Carnival Princess of Medway' at the age of thirteen, after my mum had come up with this inspired poem: 'To be the princess would be the best / I'd love to join the procession in a beautiful dress.' I was paraded through the streets of Rochester in my A-line frock and sensible flat black shoes, clutching an enormous bouquet, with a crown of roses in my hair and a fixed grin on my face. When I was sixteen I went one better and was named a *Medway Standard* Stunner! A local photographer who worked for the *Medway Standard* used to teach amateur photographers and would pay models £60 to pose for his lessons on taking portraits – something I was happy to do. He then had the bright idea of persuading the paper to sponsor a competition to find the four most stunning girls – these lucky winners would be taken on a week's swimwear shoot to Portugal. And for some reason my mum let me go to Portugal aged sixteen, with a few other girls to have our photos taken in swimwear by a group of amateur photographers, men none of us had ever met before, on the beach! Not that anything happened. In fact, I'd go so far as to say I learned a tiny bit about posing in a bikini, although in reality not enough, and had a great time with a gang of rather older glamour girls who were supportive and encouraged me to go for it.

So I was wet behind the ears perhaps when I arrived at the photo shoot in a draughty Brompton Road studio. And I was still a little naive. Fortunately, the first person I met was the fabulous Gary Cockerill. He was about twenty-five years old at the time and had been a coal-miner living in Yorkshire until he realized he was gay and wanted to become a make-up artist, so he'd come to London to try and make it. He was wonderful and the most talented guy I had ever met. He was funny and naughty and I adored him. I still do. As I stood there, he slowly looked me over, narrowing his eyes.

'You look a little bit like Cindy Crawford,' he said. 'Let's see what I can do with you.'

And he started painting on these big eyes using huge amounts of shadow, giving me massive eyebrows and lining my lips, filling them out with as much lipstick as he could get his hands on. Finally, he put a little mole on my face and backcombed the hell out of my hair. He looked pleased. I didn't recognize myself at all. He had literally painted on a face.

In those early days, I had the face of a schoolgirl with the body of a porn star and I had no idea what I was doing. I think that was probably part of my appeal, this gormless face and this porn-star body. I didn't know how to be sexy or to smize – that slightly being-sexy-with-your-eyes-narrowed pose that looks either as if you're about to break wind or you've got a bad case of conjunctivitis. I was useless. I was just going through the motions. Thankfully, Gary saw something else. He was smart, painting on the Cindy Crawford face with all the contouring and the big eyes and the lashes and the backcombed hair. He turned me into 'Glamour Girl Cindy Crawford'!

We did the test shots, along with my juvenile attempts at posing, and when we looked through them with a loop and a light box back at the agency, Samantha really liked them. I have to say I wasn't blown away. All I could see was a lot of make-up and a very curvy teenager with plenty of long hair. Frankly, I looked a little bit chubby, but I suppose I was quite sweet, as all sixteen-year-olds are. But it was hardly some photographic eureka moment during which the whole room held their breath and marvelled at my gorgeousness. We all simply chose a couple of pictures and the agency put a book together and told me they'd send me out on castings.

And then I waited. I waited and waited. Once I'd left school in the summer, I used to come into London every day, as I didn't really know what else to do with myself, and every day I'd fare-dodge. Not because I wanted to, but because I had to. There was a fast train from Chatham to London that took forty-five minutes, but I couldn't risk that one. I used to take the slow one instead. It took two and a half hours, but I reasoned if I was caught, I'd be closer to town when they threw me off. Or I could lie and say that I'd got on at Tunbridge Wells rather than Ashford, which was a lot less expensive. So I'd only have to find £7 rather than £15. I had no money. I was completely skint. I remember always being freezing, shivering on the train, because I didn't have a good coat.

But I figured anything was better than sitting on the sofa eating toast and watching daytime TV. It was lonely during the day, especially once my brother joined the army. My friends were doing their A levels, and my parents were out at work. I thought if I hung out at the agency and they saw my face, I was more likely to get work. So I'd turn up every day and be bubbly, fun, just in case anything came in, any opportunity, any castings, anything. I was always available. I would work for free, for any photographer, doing shoots or test shots, adding to my portfolio. I did whatever I could to be out of Kent and in London. I was desperate not to be back there, living with my mum and dad.

After a few months, I got a call from Samantha, who said Jeany Savage, a photographer at the *Daily Star*, was taking some really great photos of girls at the moment and would I like to meet her? She'd discovered Melinda Messenger, who was huge but had now left to work for the *Sun*. It was a big deal. Jeany was furious that the *Sun* had pinched 'her girl'. She was apparently saying she needed to find someone bigger and better; she was not going to let the *Sun* take her number-one girl without a fight! She'd put the word out that she wanted to see any new girls on the scene, and I was new.

So I turned up, still with the long hair and a bit chubby. Jeany was shooting someone else when I arrived at the studio in Chalk Farm and Gary, thankfully, was there too. He was as charming as ever and could see I was nervous. He was so positive and kept on saying that Jeany would take the best photos of me and that he was so glad I was there, that I was in the right hands. He could not have been sweeter. As soon as Jeany had finished shooting, she turned her attention to me. She had this thick blonde hair and a voice that could stop a truckload of navvies on a stag night. She was like a mad Jack Russell in wedge shoes and tight jeans, and every other word was 'fuck'. I loved her.

'All right?' she said, looking me up and down. 'Come to the toilet and show us yer tits.'

I was a bit taken aback and tried to explain that I was not there to do topless modelling, that I wanted to be an actress, but she was having none of it. She bustled me into the toilet, closed the door and waited.

'Let's have a look at 'em,' she said, nodding at my chest. 'Go on.'

She was another woman; I didn't think it mattered too much, so I lifted up my sweater.

'Oh,' she said, taking a close look. 'You've got great

tits. They're real, aren't they?' I nodded in agreement. Yes, they were. 'D'you know what you should do?'

'What?' I asked.

'Topless.' She shook her head. 'It's a waste otherwise, a terrible waste.'

So I explained again that I was seventeen, had been to Italia Conti and had sent off my CV and headshots to acting agents and that was what I eventually wanted to do, given the opportunity, and I would never be doing Page Three.

'Yeah, yeah,' she nodded. 'Let's do the shots.'

So we went back into the studio and Gary got to work again, doing my make-up in the same Cindy Crawford way as before, with the mole and the eyebrows and the big pouty lips, and Jeany took a Polaroid and looked at the photo.

'Oh bollocks,' she pronounced, staring at the picture. 'Your 'air's too long.'

And that was that. The next day, she paid for me to go and get my hair cut in a salon in Knightsbridge. It was the poshest place I had ever been to in my life. There were leather chairs, racks of glossy magazines, plus free coffee and biscuits! They cut my waist-length hair to just under my shoulders, and under Jeany's instructions gave me blonde highlights, to make me look like Cindy Crawford. Jeany had this vision and she wanted me to have a very specific look. I rather liked my long dark brown hair, but no one else did! In photos, it looked flat, so they lifted it with highlights to make it look like I had a thick and more lustrous mane.

A few days later, I went back to Chalk Farm. Gary was there again, in charge of the brushes, and Jeany was there with her enormous ring flash, and we did a sort of Cindy Crawford meets Raquel Welch shoot. It was April 1997.

My first shoot turned out to be one of the most risqué I have ever done. I don't know whether I was in a hurry or just very keen to get something, anything off the ground. I had been with the agency for months and nothing was really happening. I didn't know what else I was supposed to get from Samantha Bond. This was my chance and I took it. So firstly I posed in a chamois leather bikini, and in the next lot of pictures, I was totally naked. You can't see anything, not so much as a nipple, but I did take off *all* my clothes, and I wore some sort of naval cap. Jeany Savage is obviously a very persuasive woman! I went from a wholesome pin-up with brown hair to a superannuated Raquel Welch in one shoot. You can see in my eyes that I didn't really know what I was doing. I don't look present in the photos; I look zoned out; my eyes are elsewhere. I was clearly not feeling 'the sexy'. It's interesting to notice that now.

When the shoot was over, after we'd put away the *One Million Years BC* bikini and the jaunty naval cap,

Jeany was straight on the phone to Dawn Neesom at the *Daily Star*.

'Fucking 'ell, Dawn, I got these pictures of Kelly,' she started, 'and she's fucking amazing and we need to get her in the fucking paper.'

For the next few minutes Jeany and Dawn discussed my impending new career, and then suddenly Jeany turned to me and said, 'Oi, Kelly, what's your surname?'

'Parsons,' I replied. 'Kelly Parsons.'

'Jesus Christ, Dawn!' she exclaimed down the phone. 'I'm going to have to fucking call you back. Parsons!' she said, putting down the phone. 'Parsons? Fucking 'ell, that's 'orrible. You've got to change that. It's shit. You'll never be a star with a name like Kelly Parsons. You can't be fucking Kelly fucking Parsons. Let's think of something else.'

Gary, Jeany and I sat in silence, furiously thinking, for the next few minutes. Every so often either Gary or I came up with a surname to which Jeany would simply reply, 'Fuck off.' Then suddenly she clicked her fingers, got up, looked at me and said, 'That's it. Kelly LeBrock!' Then she clicked her fingers again. 'You can be Kelly Brook. Kelly fucking Brook. I'm calling Dawn.'

The next day, I appeared on Page Three of the *Daily Star* and made tabloid history! I was the first Page Three girl not to be showing her nipples – dressed only in a cap and massive amount of lipstick – and I was called

Kelly Brook. Kelly Parsons was no more. And there was this pneumatic pin-up in her place, with the face of a child and the body of a porn star. The tabloids went mad.

The following day, I was on the front page of the *Daily Star* in the *One Million Years BC* bikini with the headline 'Kel the New Mel' and Samantha Bond's phone started to ring.

I was now a fully fledged glamour girl. A career move that so horrified my old headmaster, Mr Vote, at Italia Conti that they held a special assembly at the school to explain to the students how this was *not* the road to take in life! I was a West End Wendy gone wrong; I'd moved over to the dark side.

Jeany Savage, on the other hand, was unbelievable. She became my mentor. She created an amazing photographic portfolio for me; she printed my pictures in a larger size than normal and presented me so glossily that I was booked for every job I went up for.

Typically during my glamour-girl days, I'd call the agency every day at 5 p.m. to see if any job or casting had come in. After a few weeks of being feted as the 'new Melinda', I remember my dad coming home, brandishing a newspaper. As a scaffolder, he was probably more exposed to the tabloid culture than most.

'Look!' he yelled. 'You're in the *Daily Sport*!'

I was mortified: there was a picture of me that some

test shoot photographer had taken and sold on to the *Daily Sport.* I was furious. So I immediately called up Samantha Bond and complained.

'Sometimes they syndicate the pictures,' she told me matter-of-factly.

'I don't want my picture syndicated,' I said. 'I don't want to be in the *Sport.* I wasn't paid for that shoot. How can someone else make money out of my image? And choose where it goes?'

I soon learned that the photographer owns the copyright of any image they take, even if that image is of you.

It was about that time I met Alan Strutt. He was a glamour photographer and also a very successful businessman. I met him at a test shoot and told him I was doing other test shoots and the photographers were selling the pictures. I said it wasn't right. He agreed, adding, 'If you only let me shoot you, I will give you seventy per cent of the income from your pictures. You will own the pictures and control where they go.'

He didn't really need the money at the time. He was a successful businessman in his own right. I think he just liked me. So he took me under his wing and started shooting me and I started earning money. He was the first person to teach me about picture syndication and copyright and owning your own pictures and controlling where they go. And I was one of the first models to syndicate their image. He really taught me how to put myself in the driving seat; if anyone deserved to make money out of photos of me, it was me.

Now I have a huge catalogue and library of pictures to which I own the copyright. So any photo that you see of me that is not a pap shot is owned by me, and I will earn money from it. A bit like record sales. I syndicate them all over the world to magazines and newspapers, and earn money from them.

When my pictures started appearing in the *Sun* and the *Star*, I was a teenager and was beginning to go out dating. My friends Lisa, Debbie, Charlotte and I would go out in Maidstone and Rochester. Sometimes we'd even step out to Hollywood's in Essex – that was a very big, cool place when I was growing up! And being a regular teenage girl, I wanted to put on the sexy dress, slap on loads of make-up, have a few Jack Daniel's and Cokes, a dance and hopefully a flirt with a boy at the end of the night. But after a while, going out with my girlfriends became a nightmare. We'd be in a bar and all the attention would suddenly be on me. Not because I was prettier than my friends, because I absolutely was not, but because I had been in the *Star* and everyone knew who I was – especially in Rochester, which is a small place. Being a lad-mag pin-up in your teens is not a good type of notoriety.

There's a particular alchemy of alcohol and testosterone that is not very attractive, and after a few drinks the men would start coming over. The brave ones would come on their own, but the cowards would come in packs: 'Are you that Kelly Brook? The one with the tits? The one off the mags?'

My girlfriends started to feel like they had to be my bodyguards when we went out, and of course they wouldn't have minded pulling or at least having a flirt themselves, but it was impossible. Where's the fun in a night out if you spend the whole time chaperoning your mate who is being lunged at left and right by silly boys who've been at the Bacardi Breezers and want to see if that bird's boobs are real? It became tiresome in the extreme.

The end result was that from a really young age I pulled back from going on girls' nights out and on holidays with my friends, missing out on being young and having fun, drinking blue cocktails in Ayia Napa or dancing like a fool in Ibiza. I am sure that is why I go out a lot now, as I never really did when I was young. I'm making up for lost time. All I did in my teens was work; I'd take the train to London and come home. I'd get on the plane and do a shoot in Venice. I'd be wandering around Germany, Paris, Vienna, going from job to job, staying in hotel rooms on my own. It was an amazing experience, but quite lonely at times.

My girlfriends weren't the only ones who did not

appreciate my new pin-up status. My electrician boy-friend at the time, Jimmy, found it equally difficult. He got into terrible fights over me. He was a very sweet, very gentle, kind boy who was a few years older than me. He was extremely protective and was always trying to treat me, give me money – £30 here, £20 there – so I could go and get an outfit in Jane Norman for a Friday night out. But he played football at the weekend and all the lads would say things like 'I saw Kel in the paper! Phwoar!' and wind him up until he'd snap. It was a lot to cope with, especially as we were so young.

In fact, the only person who was entirely comfort-able with it all was my mum. She said that the photos of me in my underwear were fabulous. I think she was thrilled that I was earning a living, and neither she nor my dad was at all judgemental. I never got the sense that she was angry or that she disapproved. I was seven-teen; it was time I went and got a job and earned some money. I do remember her sticking up for me once in the David Copperfield pub when, after a few drinks, another woman accosted her.

'Are you happy your daughter is doing all that in the newspaper?' she asked. 'Posing in her underwear? At her age?'

My mother slowly put down her drink and then pro-ceeded to have a massive fight. My mother can be quite protective sometimes, especially when she's got the bit between her teeth. I don't think anyone asked her opinion on my career again.

My contemporaries at the time were Melinda Messenger, Emma Noble and Jordan, aka Katie Price. A typical day would be Melinda, Emma, Jordan and me doing a shoot for the *Sun* in football kit as a way of cheering on 'our boys' for an England match. All the girls were lovely. The only competitive one was Katie. I remember interviewing her for some small television job on cable and she rang up the Samantha Bond agency screaming, 'Why is Kelly interviewing me? It should be the other way round!' Samantha was shocked and called me immediately to warn me that Katie was on her way and was not pleased about the interview.

I am not sure why she would sometimes be unpleasant about me behind my back, because to my face she has always been as nice as pie. I've often thought that perhaps she was in the wrong world. All the other glamour girls had big boobs, while she didn't. She was in the glamour world but with a figure for fashion. She has a lovely figure but with no hips or curves so while the rest of us were trying to tone it down, she was always trying to work it up. After a few years of not doing brilliantly in the business, she had the first of a number of boob jobs that have taken her from a 32B to a 32FF.

Sometimes the glamour world was not a great world to be moving in. I was seventeen and the male photographers were often quite a lot older. No one escorted you to shoots, or came with you, and occasionally some of them were quite skanky. I remember once turning up and it was for a catalogue. Often the catalogues were fine – you'd put on some lingerie and a couple of baby-dolls and that would be that. But sometimes they'd have a sex-toy section and the last thing I wanted was to be smizing sexily while holding a pair of fur-lined handcuffs. This time I walked into the studio and had a bad feeling, so I asked to have a look at the catalogue and it was full of vibrators. I remember that Katie was there, already in her underwear.

'I am sorry – there's been a mistake,' I said politely, turning to leave, only for Katie to shout after me, 'Oi! You! Where do you think you're going?'

We were never mates. She obviously has a sweet side to her character but I felt as if, around me at least, she would be brash and common for the sake of being brash and common. She seemed to like nothing more than saying something shocking in the hope of a reaction. Years later, I remember bumping into her at Geri Halliwell's birthday party and she was still the same Katie. I was with Danny Cipriani at the time, who I'd been dating for a couple of years. She clocked him and clearly fancied him and came over and said something so lewd we were both left slack-jawed. (Needless to say, Danny went on to go out with her a few years later!)

Both Melinda and Emma were very down to earth. Melinda was older than the rest of us and had a long-term boyfriend, Wayne, who came everywhere with her. So she was very quiet and well behaved. She wasn't in Page Three for long. She went into telly and used it very much as a stepping stone to other things. And Emma was similar. She had *The Price Is Right* going on and her relationship and marriage to James Major.

At the time, the world of glamour and lads' mags was at its height. Journalist Sean O'Hagan had recently coined the term 'new lad'; *Maxim* had launched; the market was flooded with blokes' mags: *Loaded*, *GQ* and *Arena*. No one could get enough of pretty girls in their underwear. And my career, post the Jeany Savage shoot, took off very quickly. I started with bread-and-butter jobs at the *Sun*, where they'd book me when they needed some sexy girls in sexy dresses to hang outside the High Court, holding a protest banner of some sort. Or a Dear Deirdre photo case story where I'd be the girl, in lingerie, on the bed, and usually the mistress! Soon I was on the front page, being sent to Kosovo and to HMS *Invincible* to cheer up the troops.

I'll never forget sitting in a sexy-Santa outfit on a Chinook helicopter flying over Kosovo with Gary Cockerill on a morale-booster for the troops. The boys in the chopper were showing off and getting all excited, saying things like 'D'you want to loop the loop?', 'Do you want to fly low over the trees?', 'Do you want to go right up in the sky?' And they took the chopper up high and then let it drop out of the sky. I'm dressed in suspenders and a fur-trimmed minidress, and Gary is screaming, 'Noooo!' in my ear, while I'm screaming, 'Yeeeeah,' in my suzzies. It was ridiculous.

My poor brother, Damian, was serving in Kosovo at the time and I was petrified I'd run into him. His army mates had my posters all over their walls, but he hadn't told any of his company that I was his sister. I think he was extremely embarrassed about the whole business, and the last thing he needed was me turning up in a fur-trimmed outfit with a Bo Peep hood for all his mates to have a lech over. We had different surnames, so that helped. But I was always worried that I'd spot him in the crowd!

By the end of my first year of modelling, I was one of the most successful glamour girls in the country. I'd appeared in *Loaded*, *GQ*, *FHM*, *Maxim* and *Arena*. I had appeared in pop videos though I wasn't tempted by a music career. Sasha was friends with an executive at Warner Brothers who asked her to bring me in as they were putting together a girl band. So I was dragged into a recording studio to make a demo. Nothing happened with Warner's but the tape was sent to Simon Cowell's music production company. We never heard back, though this was to give me a panicky moment many years later . . .

Sasha wanted me to keep trying but my heart wasn't in it. I already realized I would earn much more as a glamour model than I would as the new Sinitta. And I liked the fact that it was regular work. It wasn't the high-end world of fashion, but I liked that I was earning money. I was also beginning to mix with different people. I started being around rich men and playboys, and it was the first time I started dating men who were not plumbers and electricians from Kent. I was newly single, having just broken up with Jimmy, my boyfriend of two years.

I got my first real taste of the jet-set world when I was signed by Foster's lager to be their Grand Prix girl, which involved doing shoots for them and hanging out on the Grand Prix circuit. Once, I was flown to Monaco and we hosted a dinner for Foster's and a big ad agency. After the dinner, I'll never forget walking down the road in Monaco back to our hotel with a girl from the PR agency when a bloke in a sports car pulled over.

'Hey, girls,' he said. 'Where are you going?'

'Back to the hotel,' I said.

'Well, we're all going to Jimmy's bar for a few drinks if you want to come?'

'No, thanks,' I replied. 'We've got to get up early tomorrow.'

He drove off and the PR said to me, 'D'you know who that was?'

'No?'

'Prince Albert of Monaco!'

I don't know if it definitely was him but the Grand Prix circuit is one of the most testosterone-fuelled environments there is. I first met Eddie Irvine in June 1998 at Silverstone. His helicopter landed on the track, he jumped out and came over to do some pictures, I stood next to him and smiled for the camera, and that was that. I never spoke to him. I never said my name. Nothing. But obviously he asked someone who I was, as somehow he got my number and called me up in the middle of a meeting. I was at Clinton's, my lawyers, discussing a contract with my agent, Paul, from Samantha Bond.

'Kelly?'

'Yes?'

'This is Eddie Irvine.'

I am afraid I was so shocked I just blurted out his name. 'Eddie Irvine? What, *the* Eddie Irvine?'

'Yes.'

'I am sorry – I can't talk. I'll call you back.' When I put the phone down, everyone just stared at me.

I left the meeting and called him back and he asked where I lived.

'Kent,' I replied.

'I live in Monaco,' he said, 'but I'd love to take you out for dinner. Is there an airport near where you live?'

I was a little stumped. 'Um, I think Rochester has an airport.'

'Can I fly my plane into Rochester Airport?'

'I'll ask my mum and call you back.'

I was not impressed; I was just freaked out. I was living at home with my mum and dad, and knew nothing of private jets, let alone if you could land one at Rochester Airport. There he was, an international superstar Formula One driver, asking me if I knew of somewhere he could land his plane to take me out to dinner. I didn't even know of a restaurant in Rochester where we could have had dinner even if he did manage to land the jet. All I was thinking was, I'd better look in the Yellow Pages. I had no game. I wasn't cool.

In the end, he gave up on finding an airport near Rochester and decided he was going to fly into London to take me out to dinner and asked where we should go. Like I knew! I had never been out to a restaurant in London. I called a few people and someone said to me that Nobu was nice. I had never even eaten Japanese in my life – I didn't even know what it was – but I booked it anyway.

So I put on a nice dress and got ready at my mum and dad's house in Rochester. I told my mum who I was going on a date with and all she said was, 'Be careful, be careful!' I think she was excited for me. This time I splashed out on the fast train to London and turned up to have dinner with an international playboy at Nobu on Park Lane.

He was already sitting in the restaurant when I arrived. I sat down and started to look at the menu. It was all sushi and sashimi and raw fish, and I thought, I have no idea what the hell anything is. I'll just order a salad. That'll be OK. So I ordered a seaweed salad, which was the most disgusting thing I had ever eaten. All Eddie kept saying was, 'You don't eat very much, do you?' as I pretended that chewing on a mouthful of salty rubber was the most normal and indeed delicious thing in the world.

It was the most awkward uncomfortable date I have ever been on. We ended up driving around London. We went to Café de Paris and discovered it was gay night. That did not stop Eddie, who no one could suggest does not love women, from enjoying himself – he loved it. Eventually, I went back to his hotel room and we had a kiss and a fumble and that was that. The next morning, his driver drove me home, and Eddie said he was going to visit his daughter, which was a bit of a shock to me. It made me realize quite how much older he was. I was just eighteen, and he was fourteen years older than me and had a child, so I'm afraid I rather backed off him.

He called me a few times after that, but we never saw each other again.

That was the first time I was seduced by an international playboy. I am not sure I did very well!

In the meantime, I changed agents. Samantha Bond had done me well, but I wanted to try and become more mainstream and get some advertising work. There are only so many times you can hang outside the High Court looking like an escapee from Benny Hill casting. So I moved to Helen Smith at Smithy's, taking Paul, who had been doing all my bookings at Samantha Bond, with me.

It turned out to be one of the worst moves I have ever made, as I worked for six months and ended up losing thousands of pounds. It was all being held back for some reason. Turns out the agency was in trouble and there were some rumours about Helen Smith's fast-living lifestyle. She was always great fun!

But she did do one thing for me. She made me go and have my teeth fixed. My mum had my teeth put in braces far too young and now they were all crooked again, so Helen took me to an orthodontist on Harley Street – Dr Didier Fillion – who put invisible tracks on, giving me a Hollywood smile. But that's all Helen really did for me!

After that I got wise. I decided to appoint a top London accountant and take hold of my own financial affairs. I felt that I had not been treated properly once with respect to my money so I did not want to let it happen again – that would have been just plain stupid. So I set up my company and from then on looked after my own affairs. It was an expensive lesson to learn.

Fortunately, I was beginning to develop some good relationships with a few production companies and an entertainment marketing company, Cutting Edge, who were packaging up celebrities with brands, for instance creating clothing lines with retailers. The company's founder, Philip Moross, became a friend. Even if I was not working, I did the same thing that I'd done at Samantha Bond and took the train to London to hang out in their reception. I just wanted to be around people who were busy and doing stuff. There was nothing going on in Rochester; it was all happening in London. I am sure that was how I got my first clothing range for Littlewoods sportswear. I was constantly hustling. I was always working, and I always had very good relation- ships with people. I'd turn up on time and never had a day off, so I started to build a good collection of clients who regularly used me.

The boys at Cutting Edge packaged me up, putting me together with a whole load of already quite well- established celebrities like Denise Van Outen and Ulrika Jonsson. They sneaked me in and somehow I managed to slip between the sheets of the contract so to speak.

I was always in reception; they had to do something with me!

I was then booked by Eidos Games for the launch of *Tomb Raider*, which was to be their biggest game. Rhona Mitra was to play Lara Croft, and I was one of the characters in *Fighting Force*. I travelled all over the States, including Atlanta and LA; we met lots of interesting people, and I earned really good money. The work was really beginning to come in by now. I did hair commercials in Turkey for Blandex. I was in Spain doing calendars for Harley-Davidson. And then finally Philip managed to get me a large contract for Triumph bras, advertising their new Flaunt bra, for the bigger-busted girl. The campaign caused a bit of a stir, mainly because of the enormous fifteen-metre-high billboard of my boobs on the A3 flyover to Heathrow! It was the largest poster in Europe. So I did finally get my Eva Herzigova moment. It had come by quite a circuitous route, but I got there. In the end.

My glamour-girl journey was an eventful one, from Carnival Princess of Medway to *Loaded* cover girl and bra pin-up. Along the way I was interviewed by Chris Evans on *TFI Friday* and I was asked to go on radio shows. I was booked to go on *The Frank Skinner Show*, but I never thought I'd made it, because I didn't really have anything to talk about. I felt a bit of a fraud who didn't really deserve to be there. I was just a bit of eye candy.

But still, these were the opportunities that were presenting themselves and I took them.

I am grateful I got in and out of glamour modelling with my dignity intact. In and out without showing my nipples! Everyone thinks the glamour world is run by predatory males who prey on innocent girls, but it's not really. It's a world full of mad old women and wonderful queens with the occasional straight bloke thrown into the mix. It's not bitchy or mean or remotely rapacious, unlike the world of television. A world I was about to enter. A world that I walked naively into with my eyes closed. A world that would almost, quite literally, eat me for breakfast.

4

Eaten for Breakfast

'You can't do that!' exclaimed my mum, when I called her up and told her I'd managed to bag one of the biggest presenting jobs on TV. 'You've never done live TV, Kel. Are you sure?'

And it seems she wasn't the only one with grave reservations. Little did I know when I secured the *Big Breakfast* job that the jury was not only out but also sharpening its knives, along with its pens. The six months I would spend hosting Channel 4's flagship show with the inimitable Johnny Vaughan would be one of the steepest, rockiest, trickiest learning curves of my life. The fact that I managed to get through it without resorting to heavy sedatives and a darkened room is something I am quite proud of. What doesn't break you, as they say . . .

And it all started so positively.

I was happily presenting numerous youth TV shows,

including the edifyingly entitled *VPL* (*Visible Panty Line*) on cable TV, the show where I had once interviewed the apparently infuriated Katie Price. I was eighteen years old and earning enough money modelling and doing promotional work. I was having fun, enjoying myself. Interviewing strippers who made their costumes out of an English breakfast, and pubic wig-makers, was entertaining enough. Then I got a call. Planet 24, Bob Geldof's production company and the makers of *The Big Breakfast*, wanted to speak to me about auditioning for the show.

I had recently changed agent again. Leaving Helen behind, I'd moved to Neil Reading, one of London's top PR men, with offices in Golden Square, Soho. His young company was going places, and he employed a lovely girl called Faye to manage both Emma Noble and me, while he took care of the PR. He had a lot of mates in the media and was extremely well connected; he knew exactly who was who and what was what.

At the time, the *Big Breakfast* job was one of the jewels in the morning-TV crown. Originally presented by Chris Evans and Gaby Roslin, with daily ratings of over two million, it was still riding high in the media consciousness and was now hosted by Johnny Vaughan and Denise Van Outen. Together, they had a hot chemistry and a smart line in repartee. It was a hip show with a groovy reputation, and now that Denise had resigned,

In the arms of my mum, Sandra, who was (and is) a petite, blonde powerhouse.

With my dad, Kenneth, when I was about three.

My cute baby brother Damian came along about eighteen months after me, and I adored him.

My glamorous nan, Ann Kelly, with my
granddad in Malaysia, where they were living.
Granddad was in the army when they married.

Mum and Dad on their wedding day, with their parents.

Me and Damian with our half-sister, Sasha, at Butlins.

BELOW: Looking like butter wouldn't melt in my mouth.

RIGHT: My first modelling photo! Striking a pose in my best clothes, outside our house. I've always loved fashion.

Messing around with Damian.

ABOVE LEFT: With Dannielle Brent, my best friend at Italia Conti.

ABOVE: A spotty teenager!

LEFT: An Italia Conti headshot – I developed early! I always looked older than my age.

RIGHT: A chorus girl in panto – here I'm front row, second from the right, in *Dick Whittington*, in 1995 at Central Theatre.

BELOW: Clearly I was a big Madonna fan as a teenager. I never imagined I'd one day meet her, though.

BELOW: All the family at home – Mum, Me, Damian, Sasha and Dad.

The picture that won me
the *Medway Standard* Stunner
competition.

Posing on the beach in Portugal,
aged sixteen – my prize for winning
the competition.

Wearing even less – my first shoot with Jeany Savage
was also one of my most risqué.

Kelly Parsons was no more. Instead, Kelly Brook was a fully fledged
glamour model. This is another Jeany Savage shot.

ABOVE LEFT: With Lisa, my best friend from Rochester.

ABOVE: Smiling at the cameras with Eddie Irvine, who'd just arrived by helicopter, at the Grand Prix Ball in Silverstone.

LEFT: Cheering up the troops in my sexy-Santa outfit, courtesy of the *Sun*.

it seemed every girl in TV-Land was up for the job. Liza Tarbuck, Davina McCall and Gail Porter were some of the most well-known names being bandied about. There were even bets on at the bookies as to who was going to step into Denise's great big shoes. My name was never mentioned. Chiefly, I suppose, because aside from some glamour girls, garages full of car mechanics, a pubic wig-maker and a nation of fifteen-year-old boys, nobody knew who I was. But Faye told me they were keen. They'd seen me in the newspapers and wanted someone sexy and fun, someone to spark off Johnny, someone who could handle him, and they thought I might fit the bill.

I was incredibly nervous but also really excited. I had nothing to lose by auditioning, although I never thought in a million years I would get the job. It was a shot in the dark. Lastly, at the end of the phone call, Faye said that due to the massive media interest, I wasn't to tell anyone, not a soul. The whole interview process was to be conducted in secret.

A few days later, a blacked-out Mercedes came to collect me from my mum and dad's in Rochester and drove me to London. I remember being taken to an underground car park and spirited into a lift so as not to be seen by anyone. It seems ridiculous, looking back, but even the meeting room had black paper on the windows so nobody in the production office could see in. After a brief handshake and a chat, I was escorted into the inner sanctum, where I was to meet Johnny Vaughan.

He was bouncing off the walls; I had never met anyone with so much energy and so much chat. He was full on and it was extremely hard to get a word in edgeways. During the first ten minutes, he told me his girlfriend was Antonia Davis, the costume designer who I'd worked with at Eidos. We'd done a trip to New York together and had kept in touch. After my name had come up in a meeting, it had apparently been Antonia who'd been very pro me for the job.

Johnny and I hit it off. Weirdly, I didn't find the tsunami of anecdotes intimidating; my childhood in the David Copperfield, surrounded by blokeish banter, had paid off! I was totally at ease. I actually forgot the cameras and producers were in the room and Johnny and I just sparred off each other. Johnny has said subsequently he wanted me for the job because I didn't scream desperation, or have that panicked 'pick me' look in my eyes. I think I must simply have been completely guileless. I had the confidence of youth and didn't really question what I was doing. It was as if I was just having a chat and I left thinking, What a lovely bunch of people.

The next week, I got the call from Neil Reading saying they wanted me to replace Denise. I was also told that Lord Waheed Alli, the head of Planet 24, wanted to take me for tea at the House of Lords, where we would chat about the show and get to know each other.

Recently made a Labour peer and in his early thirties, Lord Alli met me at the entrance to the House of Lords in full ermine regalia. I am still not sure if he was dressing to impress or if he'd come fresh from a vote or a debate, or perhaps he just fancied wearing some fur. I have to admit the cloak was stunning, but the whole effect was rather intimidating. I remember following him as he billowed along the long corridors towards the tea room, thinking, I left school two years with not a pot to piss in and now, here I am, being taken to tea by a member of the peerage and about to sign my first TV contract for one of the most sought-after jobs in the country.

En route to the tea room, we walked through a specially carpeted area only lords are allowed to walk on; us mere mortals have to trot on the floor alongside, which I found very entertaining! But I was tense. Despite what Johnny thought, I did need this break more than anything. This was going to take me from glamour girl to legitimate television personality. Films and acting were still my ambition, but I knew this was a stepping stone to where I wanted to be.

Waheed ordered a delicious cream tea, and he and I chatted about the show, Johnny and Denise, and my background. I was fascinated to learn how he became a

91

member of the House of Lords. I really liked him. He then started to talk about Neil Reading. I explained I had lost money with my previous modelling agent, Helen Smith, and that my good friend Philip Moross had suggested I work with Neil and so far I was very happy. I was in the press an awful lot at that time, as Neil had a fantastic relationship with the tabloids. That was really his world. He was not a television agent.

As the conversation continued, I started to get the impression that Neil Reading made Waheed and the producers of *The Big Breakfast* very nervous. I knew they wanted to keep the announcement secret and were probably not sure if they could trust Neil not to leak the news. To be fair, I think they would have felt the same about any PR who had such a good relationship with the press. Waheed went on to say that if they thought it appropriate, and if they felt he was leaking stories to the press, they would expect me to fire Neil Reading. I was in shock. Neil and Faye were my agents and so far had been wonderful. I was in a dilemma; I was very inexperienced and had no idea what to do. This was all a little sophisticated and media-playing-media for me. I wanted to please Waheed and understood his concern, but on the other hand, I felt ambushed by this conversation and also felt it would be very sneaky and underhand for me to reach this kind of agreement about my agent behind his back. But I didn't want to lose the job; it was an opportunity and I had to be ruthless and just go for it.

I never spoke to Neil about this, and thankfully, it never was an issue. Neil looked after me throughout my stint on *The Big Breakfast* and for some time after. I never once felt I couldn't trust him, and even to this day I think he is one of the smartest, most well-connected PRs in London.

My deal with *The Big Breakfast* was done, both of them, and I was introduced to Su Judd, the wardrobe mistress on the show. This was the first time I was going to be dressed for a living and I was excited. The producers were wary of where I had come from and didn't want to turn off the female audience by making me overtly sexy and having my boobs spilling out everywhere at 7 a.m. So they issued a strict no-cleavage policy, and my skirts were to come below the knee. They wanted me to appear very girl next door and not at all threatening.

Su Judd had a great eye and great taste, and took me to Manolo Blahnik to buy shoes. It was a tiny boutique off the King's Road, and I remember spending a small fortune on a cute pair of red and blue polka-dot heels. We then walked round to the famous clothes shop Voyage. It was close to my old stomping ground, the Samantha Bond agency, and previously I had only ever pressed my face against the window, like some fashion-starved Tiny Tim. I had never dared press the bell. They apparently only let you in if they liked the look of you or knew you, as Madonna, who was once famously said to have been turned away, found out. It was a velvet-edged treasure chest of diamanté-trimmed cardigans and pearlized pieces. I was like a little girl in a sweet shop.

Spurred on, I suppose, by the producers' new chaste image of myself, I decided to restyle my hair. The Cindy Crawford locks had to go if I wanted the girls to like me. The idea was for my image to be as far away from a glamour model as possible. I remember my nan finding this idea very puzzling indeed. She couldn't get her head around the librarian jumpers and sensible skirts. 'Why are you covering up your lovely figure?' she asked me. Later, I told the story to Johnny, who of course got me to repeat it live on air. And so a campaign to 'sex up Kelly' was born!

First came the dry runs of the show. The studio, 2 Lock Keepers' Cottages, was an East End house with a kitchen, bedroom and living area that appeared to have been decorated by nursery-school kids on a sugar high; it was so bright and zany and awash with fluoro colours you needed sunglasses to cope with it first thing in the morning. The show was furiously fast-paced and changed at the drop of a cue card; it wasn't so much scripted as made up as it went along. For someone who had had zero experience of live television, it was a baptism of fire.

The dry runs were being streamed through to Channel 4 so they could oversee what I was doing, and Andi Peters, who was working at the channel at the time and kept a close eye on proceedings, told me I was doing fine. But the learning curve was massive.

Initially, I was just myself; I told a few crude jokes that went down extremely badly. I was a silly teenager who had no idea about libel or PC or very much anything else to be honest. I remember hearing screams of protest from the producers in my earpiece. (Something else that was entirely new to me!) I realized pretty quickly a lot of my jokes and banter were not appropriate for morning telly and that I would have to smarten up my act and 'bring it down a notch'.

When it was finally announced at the beginning of January 1999 that I was to take over from Denise, we held a photocall at the studio and I did a press junket, trying to get all the media on side. The following day, I was on the cover of the *Sun* with the headline 'Kelly-vision: Model Gets *Big Breakfast* Job'. It was accompanied by a picture of me in lingerie that Alan Strutt had taken. He couldn't sell enough pictures of me; he was delighted. Syndication was in overdrive. And I got my first taste of what it was like to be a celebrity.

I had photographers camped outside my parents' house, and the telephone rang endlessly. My mum thought it was hilarious and made pots of tea for everyone standing at the end of our lawn. I received hundreds of bouquets of flowers, some from friends, others from colleagues, some from people I had not seen in years and others still from people I had never met before. I even received a nice Interflora bouquet from the manager at the local Asda. I took it all in my stride. Even the post that was barely addressed: 'Kelly Brook, Kent'. It didn't occur to me that it was insane or unusual; it was just what was happening. It's what I thought I wanted.

The show went live on 1 February 1999, when I was nineteen. My first week was fantastic. The producers had asked me to come up with a list of people I'd like to interview to help ease me into it all. I had always wanted to meet Kathy Burke and Brenda Blethyn, who were two of my favourite actresses of all time, and I was also keen to interview my old school friends from Italia Conti, Dannielle Brent, who was in *Bad Girls* at the time, and Natasha Green, who was starring in *Hollyoaks*.

They were all brilliant and turned up on the show. It was like a dream come true. I was having the time of my life. I had new clothes, I had been given a car, plus a driver, and I was interviewing my friends and idols on national television. I couldn't believe my luck. In the first month, I interviewed Hugh Grant, Britney Spears, Ricky Martin, Eminem and Beyoncé. I was enjoying myself hugely. The show was so alive and unpredictable.

One morning, I remember being screamed at by the gallery to move to the left during a segment in the *Big Breakfast* garden. 'Left!' they yelled in my ear, as I gently winced. 'Left! *Left!*' It was only later I discovered that a corpse the police were trying to rescue from the river behind me had bobbed through the shot.

It took just over a month for my honeymoon period to end. On 11 March, the negative stories began.

One of the problems, and I am the first to admit there were many, was that no one thought I deserved to be there. I hadn't 'given'. I hadn't earned it. I wasn't a DJ on local radio, or a journalist who'd languished for years on a local newspaper. I had done a year of pretty poor-quality cable TV and that was it. I was essentially a glamour girl who'd got lucky, and no one liked that.

And secondly, I wasn't very good! I found the machinations of live TV hard. It was difficult to talk while someone was screaming in your ear, and I also found the way things could chop and change at the last minute hard to handle. I was young and inexperienced.

We never had an autocue on the show; it was scripted using large cards scrawled on in marker pen that were held by runners, who'd stand either side of the camera. But Johnny was always improvising and going off message. I liked that – it made it spontaneous – but it was difficult to keep up. Sometimes during a live show Johnny would shout around and be very funny for so long that the thirty-second link that'd been written for me to read would suddenly be reduced to ten seconds. Then a producer would start shouting in my ear.

'Kelly? Kelly? All right, Kelly, make that link ten seconds. Ten. Now! You! Ten seconds! Wrap it up, Kelly. Wrap it *up*!'

So the runner who was holding the card, who was seventeen and was also on his first job, would hear the producer, grab the card, put a line through the link and rewrite the outro. I'd be standing there trying to read some seventeen-year-old's panicked handwriting while trying to be effortless, glamorous and fun at the same time. And frankly, it threw me. I'd be squinting at the scrawled lines and saying something like 'Coming up next week is Susan. Or is that Sam? Or Sarah?'

It was too hard. Whereas if Johnny couldn't read it he would just say something, anything, any old crap that came into his head. But I'd panic and look like a rabbit in the headlights; I was even christened dyslexic because I couldn't read. Obviously, I could read; I just couldn't read their writing.

My supposed illiteracy did become farcical at one point, when Anthea Turner called my mum at the house. Apparently she did a lot of work with the Dyslexic Society and she wanted to reach out and help me in my hour of need. She wanted to soften the pain. My mother was a little bit put out at first, but in the end she was thrilled that a celebrity had called our house.

All I was doing was trying my best. Every morning before the show, I would sit with Caroline, the producer, and run through the script. I sometimes found the writers' turn of phrase difficult – I was a working-class girl from Rochester and the scriptwriters tended to be university educated. They were very attuned to Johnny's style as they'd been working with him for years but I was new so I politely asked if maybe they could listen to how I spoke and try to write more for me. I also asked if they could make the script less complicated, more like bullet points of the information they wanted to get across, so then I would have the chance to use my own words and hopefully my personality would come through.

Anyway, unbeknown to me, somehow the note to the writers and producers about writing for me got leaked to the newspapers. All of a sudden a small article appeared in the *Telegraph* saying that I wanted scripts to be kept minimal and that certain words like 'intrepid' were causing me to slip up. Everyone else followed suit. I was christened 'Calamity Kelly' in the *Daily Mail* and from that moment on it was like a witch-hunt. *Heat* magazine, who'd just launched their first issue with me licking Johnny's cheek on the cover, commissioned a journalist to sit and watch the show every day for a week and make notes of my alleged cock-ups. On a live TV show, there were going to be a few.

The drip, drip, drip of negative press continued. The show was on between 7 and 9 a.m. 5 days a week, and on top of that I was doing a lot of PR for the show and was still modelling during the day; I was exhausted. Trying to go to bed early in my parents' house was virtually impossible. No matter how many times I shouted and begged, our house didn't sleep until 11 p.m. I was supposed to be in bed by 7 p.m. to be up at 4 a.m., but that never happened. Sometimes I didn't even get home until after 9 p.m. So I used to try and sleep in the cab on the way home, and out of desperation I asked the cab company to ask their drivers not to talk to me so that I could lie on the back seat with my mouth open, dribbling gently onto my shoulder. Also there are only so many times you can answer the question 'So what's that Johnny Vaughan like?' After the fourth time that week, I'd be thinking *please* just let me kip. Unfortunately, like most things going on at the time, my request was misconstrued and one evening when I got into the car to be taken home after a long day, the driver said, 'I've been told not to talk to you.' Which of course made me sound like a right old diva, which was not how it was meant.

I began to dread the morning car journeys too. When my driver, Tony, used to collect me, there was always a pile of newspapers in the car I had to read for work. It was rare that there wasn't some scathing piece on me. Usually written by a woman. It was bullying like I had never experienced before. Some days it made it very difficult to be upbeat and go on live TV and host a show, knowing as I did that powerful people in the media had it in for me. For no real reason. They only had to turn over to *GMTV* if they thought I was that appalling. But people were not turning over. The show had great ratings, so the media perception was not accurate. It put the producers in a terrible dilemma. I was doing well on the show and we were getting the ratings, although you wouldn't have known it. The press we were generating was so negative. They even used to play around with the figures. They'd compare our 7 a.m. ratings (which was the lowest point of any show) with Johnny and Denise's 8.15 a.m. ratings (always the highest part of the show) so that ours looked much worse than the previous ones. We couldn't do anything right.

The person I felt sorry for most was Johnny. He'd had so much success with Denise, and I think he was a bit angry that his livelihood was being threatened. The perception in the media was that because Denise had left, the show was now shit. And he was thinking, Wait a minute, Denise was on the show before I turned up and it wasn't great. I was the person who turned this around and now I am getting stick. So I think he was a little pissed off, and I'm pretty sure the crew were. They were all such a gang, and they were very much Johnny's gang. They'd been together long before I arrived and I remember feeling that they'd be there long after I went. They all had nicknames – Cockney Vic, Carpet Monster, Ruff Bird – and they had a shared history and shared jokes. They were very much Team Johnny.

In fact, the only silver lining at this moment was that Alan and I were making a fortune out of my demise. Every piece about my illiteracy, my incompetence or my diva-like behaviour was accompanied by a sexy shot of me in my underwear. But after a while, I started losing the stomach for it and stopped selling my own pictures unless we checked what the story was about first. I still do that now, but if I have learned one thing over time, it is that newspapers can be somewhat economical with the truth. More often than not they'll say one thing and then print another. They don't write the truth; they write the story they want to tell, the story they know will sell the most copies, as I remember only too well when I did my first *TV Times* shoot for *The Big Breakfast*. I arrived in the studio to find that they'd built a rocket and I remember saying, 'Oh, OK. That's great. What's the shoot about?' And they replied, 'Well, you're new on *The Big Breakfast* and we want to do a shoot about Kelly rocketing to success!'

'Rocketing to success.' It sounded perfect, just what I

wanted to hear. So I said, 'Amazing!' and I got on the rocket, straddled the thing, and then the following week I saw the photos and the piece, with the headline 'Kelly Brook: I'm No Rocket Scientist'. It just goes to show how they can change something so quickly.

It was the perfect rise-and-fall story. It's typical of the UK media to build up a show only to knock it down. You can hardly blame the press really. I was a gift. They are always keen to put a girl in a bikini on the front page because it shifts copies. Negative scandalous stories also shift copies. But negative scandalous stories about a girl in a bikini – that was press gold dust. At the time, I was the perfect media storm.

Although, there was one woman who was on my side: Sue Carroll from the *Mirror* was the only journalist who was kind to me. Despite the make-down, the dowdy hair and the Miss Moneypenny outfits, the middle-aged media harridans were still after me, but Sue was lovely. She was the only female journalist who wrote positive things, and she really came on board and tried to change people's perceptions. She asked me if I had any school reports that were good, or showed I had any qualifications, because the image I had was one of total stupidity and she was trying to change that. She continued to be supportive, writing big profile pieces about me right up until the point that she passed away from cancer a few years ago. I will never forget her kindness and what a fantastically glamorous lady and truly great journalist she was. I loved our lunches at Joe Allen.

The only other person who was really on my side was Jason Statham.

I'd met Jason in the summer of 1998 on Santorini. I was there for a photo shoot for my own Littlewoods range and I remember on the first night having a funny feeling that something profound was going to happen. It was very odd, and then someone said to me that because Santorini was a volcanic island, it was rumoured to be quite powerful. I have since heard that all your emotions are supposed to be focused and magnified on the island; it is said to have magical powers.

After dinner, the team and I went to a bar where we'd heard all the male models who were doing a Speedo shoot were going to be. Jason was also a high-board diver on the British National Diving Team at the time, and eleven years older than me. When I saw him, I thought he was the photographer, as he had a bald head, a broken nose and was quite short. He couldn't possibly be a model.

'You know my ex-girlfriend,' he said.

I did. She was a model and we'd worked together on a job once. Jason and I got chatting and he had a really husky voice and I thought he was fabulous. We had a real connection. He wasn't at all like a himbo male model; he was a charming rogue. That night, he left early because he was hung-over, so toxed and tired from boozing the night before.

I didn't see much more of him until I went back to London. I was hanging out in Cutting Edge when Philip Moross came down and told me that Jason had just made this film, *Lock, Stock and Two Smoking Barrels*, with a bloke called Guy Ritchie (which had yet to be released) and they were all thinking of making some more films and that Matthew Vaughn, the producer, wanted to meet me.

So I toddled off to Scar Films, which was nearby, and met Matt, who was so posh and plummy and sweet. I could tell that he quite liked me and so I told him I wanted to be an actress. Then he said that Jason was round the corner and my eyes must have lit up, so he rather charmingly suggested we went and said hello. I remember Jason looking quite stunned when I walked into the cafe with Matt. There was definitely an alpha-male moment between them when they both looked each other up and down like a couple of silverback gor-illas. I realized immediately that these were two blokes who enjoyed winding each other up. They really were, and are, chalk and cheese. Although they loved each other, during this whole period there were moments when they just didn't see eye to eye.

I never had any interest in Matt. He was way too posh and successful for me. I have always liked the rogues, and it was fabulous to see Jason again. We had a proper chat and he asked me if I wanted to go on a date. His mate Piers Adam had a club in Fulham and I remember driving up from Rochester in my red Peugeot 106 and going for dinner and then out to the club.

On one of our first dates, he turned up in a battered blue Astra van and told me it was his brother's. It wasn't. It was his. The windows wouldn't shut. There was no heating or stereo. It was clear he had no money, but that didn't stop him from behaving like a real gent. He took me on numerous dates, and I was wined and dined. But I adored him. It was clear he had a lot going for him. He was talented and fun and going places. At the time, he was something of a chancer. A little bit of this, a little bit of that. He lived in South London but he was from Great Yarmouth, where his dad was a market trader. When he was younger Jason had made money doing mock auctions, which are a bit like street theatre. You set up a market stall and, using a microphone, build up a big audience, luring them in with the promise of eye-wateringly good deals for your miracle shammy leather, getting the crowd worked up. Eventually, it becomes a feeding frenzy. Jason said to me once that all you are doing is appealing to people's greed, and if they think they are going to get something for nothing, they will stop at very little to do just that.

Guy Ritchie saw him in a French Connection advert

and asked him to audition for *Lock, Stock*. During the audition, he told Guy all about his mock auctions and Guy loved it so much he put it in the film. So *Lock, Stock* opens with Jason and a suitcase and a whole load of street-market banter.

It was at the end of September 1998 at Steve Coogan's opening night of his West End stand-up show *The Man Who Thinks He's It* at the Theatre Royal, Drury Lane, when Guy and Matt realized Jason and I were going out with each other. We had kept it very much under the radar. I was still eighteen, while he was twenty-nine and I think our age difference concerned Jason a little. We didn't do the red carpet together. Not that there was much opportunity for that sort of thing at the time, but Jason was not that kind of bloke. There was nothing he disliked more than standing and posing next to his girl-friend on the red carpet. It bored him to tears. He was not interested in the press or the paparazzi or clothes or anything like that. Having said that, he wasn't a thug devoid of aesthetic – he had impeccable taste when it came to architecture and furniture – but clothes and being photographed made his eyes glaze over.

Even when *Lock, Stock* was nominated for a BAFTA he didn't manage to do the red carpet very successfully. I had been on *The Big Breakfast* for a couple of months by then and it was the first time the paps were scream-ing my name. It was madness. The boys had been nominated for an Orange Audience Award and it was the first taste that any of us had really had of that sort of flashbulb frenzy. Jason and I walked down the red carpet as quickly as we could. We didn't stop for pictures because we didn't know we were supposed to: we didn't know what to do! Our hands were shaking as we were being screamed at. All we thought was, This is hell and embarrassing. Let's just get inside quickly. The next day, someone asked why we didn't stop for pictures and it was because we didn't have a publicist to tell us what to do. We had no idea.

The *Lock, Stock* wave was extraordinary. They won the Audience Award that night and we had a huge party. They were all on such a big ride and it was a privilege to be a tiny part of it. All these boys were going somewhere fast. Jason, Vinnie, Guy, Matthew, they were on a different level and were untouchable; everyone wanted a piece of them. They were so handsome and talented. Their mate Piers Adam had just started opening up all his clubs and bars. Guy was constantly on the phone to a girl called Madge, who I later found out was Madonna, but everyone called her Madge for the first couple of months. It never occurred to me to question who they were talking about. Guy was keeping it all on the down low.

Guy had been dating Tania Strecker but now there was Madge on the scene. Perhaps that's one of the reasons why Madonna liked him so much, because he had been unavailable.

I remember one weekend I'd been given a free Honda HRV and Sting and Trudie offered Guy their house for the weekend, as they were not going to be there. So Guy, Tania, Jason and I all drove down in my car to Sting's house in Wiltshire. It was the most amazing house I had ever seen. It was an organic farm, with hot and cold running staff and a small house on the lake. It was so beautiful. None of us could believe it. We thought we'd made it. Here we were, Jason and me, a couple of chavs, in Sting's house. It was fabulous!

Trudie loved all those boys, particularly Jason Flemyng and Guy and Matthew. She'd put money into *Lock, Stock* and was one of the producers. She was brilliant. Sting was also in the film, right at the end. It was a very interesting mixture of posh and wide boys, and a very nice gang of people: Guy and the stunningly leggy Tania; Jason Flemyng, who had been with the actress Lena Headey for years; and Matt, who had started to go out with a lovely PR girl called Tanya Bard. They were golden times. The boys were in demand and there was such a buzz about them. We were a little gang. And then Vinnie Jones would rock up and occasionally send the whole thing over the edge, creating chaos and fun and a massive party. Sadly, the only person who wasn't there was Nick Moran, who had fallen out with Guy. I really liked Nick. He was going out with Sienna Guillory at the time, who also became a good friend of mine.

The job on *The Big Breakfast* did make me feel that I could bring something to the table; I was getting invited to these events on my own merit. Quite a lot of the time I would just meet the boys there. I wasn't simply a glamour model; I was doing well and had my own thing going on. But Jason wasn't actually working at the time. He didn't work for a couple of years after *Lock, Stock* came out. Although he was riding the wave, the film offers were yet to materialize.

So when I suggested we go on holiday to Gran Canaria for two weeks in the sunshine and to see his parents, who had lived there for years, Jason was available to come. I was exhausted. I'd been in the eye of the *Big Breakfast* storm for six months and was desperate for some sun, sangria and a snooze.

For the first couple of days we just lay by the pool and did absolutely nothing. It was bliss. The early starts and the endless afternoon promo events had really taken their toll. I wanted to zone out and recharge completely so that I could come back and face the fray with renewed vigour. Then on day five of the holiday, I went for a walk along the beach, leaving Jason asleep in the sun, and thought I would go and pick up a newspaper, as it would be lovely to have a gentle read over lunch. It was 28 July 1999. I wandered into the newsagent's and there on the front cover of the *Sun* was a stock photo of me in my Triumph underwear with the headline 'TV Kelly Axed: *Big Brekkie* girl goes after just six months'.

I was so shocked. I couldn't believe it. This was the first that I'd heard about it. As far as I was concerned, I was simply on holiday, taking a break. I knew they had lined up Sara Cox to fill in while I was gone, but I was supposed to go back. I had Will Smith to interview on Monday, or so I thought. I was devastated.

I walked back down the beach and woke up Jason and we sat reading the piece together on the sand. It was all there, my inability to read, my stumbling over long words, the lack of chemistry between Johnny and me, the plummeting ratings. It was awful. I could feel my confidence being crushed and ground out of me. I couldn't understand it. I had gone from 'Kellyvision' to 'TV Kelly Axed' in six months.

I called my mum. She reread the piece to me down the phone, adding her own particularly fruity commentary, and then at the end she said, 'Fuck 'em, Kel. You can't go back there.' And she was right. The knives were out and I was so unprotected I couldn't possibly walk back into that fluoro building in the East End and look everyone in the eye again. It looked as if someone had been speaking to the press and I felt as if I simply had no idea who I could trust. The irony, of course, was that after all the toing and froing and cream cakes with Lord

Alli, Neil Reading hadn't leaked a thing. My representation had been nothing but professional and cooperative. I felt badly let down by Planet 24.

So I called them up and resigned. They made rather weak attempts to keep me, asking me to be a roving reporter, something along the same lines as Richard Bacon, but I couldn't do that. Ed Forsdick, the producer, did call me and was quite upset about everything. Ultimately I think they wanted to do the right thing and come to some sort of arrangement. I got on with everyone and it wasn't as if I was a bitch who everyone was trying to get rid of. But it wasn't to be. Oddly, Ed was the only one to call me back. No one else from Planet 24 ever contacted me afterwards, and I was never invited to tea at the House of Lords again.

It was a really tough time. I was back to square one. I was bruised and didn't really know what my next step should be.

Meanwhile, Johnny was teamed up with various replacements, Sara Cox and Liza Tarbuck among them. Eventually, they chose Liza.

Liza and Johnny had been mates for years and she was quite a lot older than me. She was funny and sharp and a great foil for Johnny, and together they changed the demographic of the show. I think there may have been a lot of politics that I was not privy to between Channel 4 and Planet 24 about who they were aiming for. They would have wanted to get the female press on board, and quite frankly, I was *not* appealing to them. As far as they were concerned, I would be forever tarnished by my lads'-mag image and they didn't like me at all. I was still a male fantasy figure, and no amount of frumpy hair and sensible clothing would win them over.

I didn't see Johnny much after that. I went to his wedding to Antonia, a month later, with Jason, but we did not keep in touch. I don't blame him really. I am sure I remind him of unhappier times. Although recently, since he's left Capital Radio, he has been in contact and has taken me out for lunch a couple of times.

So there I was, tired and fired in Gran Canaria, about to take the plane home, when I suddenly realized there might be photographers at the airport. Just before we boarded, I said to Jason, 'Come on, let's go and buy some enormous sombreros so we look like we're having fun.' I didn't want to look like I was down. I didn't want it to look like they'd won.

I never took the exalted heights of 'Kellyvision' seriously, so I decided not to take 'TV Kelly Axed' that seriously either. I arrived at Heathrow with a great big ridiculous hat on my head and a fixed grin on my face. If Italia Conti had taught me anything, it was how to handle rejection and failure, and here I was handling them both. All I needed were the maracas! The press might have kicked me about for six months, but they hadn't won. I was still standing – still standing and wearing a stupid hat!

I never really thought *The Big Breakfast* was the be all and end all. I remember sitting there thinking that I wanted to be the one being interviewed. I wanted to be interviewed about the movie I'd made. I didn't want to be the person asking the questions about how fabulous someone else's life was; I wanted to be the one answering them.

I never set out to be a TV presenter. It wasn't something I imagined I'd be doing; it wasn't something I'd hankered after. It had fallen into my lap, a gift from the gods that in reality turned out to be something of a poisoned chalice. All I really wanted to do was act. And six months later, I got the chance.

Ironically, I was asked to go back onto *The Big Breakfast*, only this time to be interviewed on their last ever show. My agent never bothered to ask me about it; she simply wrote back a note: 'Sorry – gone to Hollywood.' A bit juvenile, I know.

5

Hollywood and the Bust-Up

It would have been more poetic if I had gone directly to Hollywood and not passed 'Go'. In fact, I went via Hammersmith and, before that, a challenging little 'fuck and chuck' role in a teenage slasher-horror film in Vancouver.

Ripper was one of those films that kind of did what it said on the tin. It was an exploitation B-movie, directed by John Eyres and starring Bruce Payne, and I learned that the first rule of the horror genre is 'Sex kills.' So if you are a girl in a short skirt dancing provocatively under the throbbing red lights of a poorly illuminated nightclub, then your time is shortly up and your death will sure as hell be grisly. Sadly, I was the one minxing around, so I was inevitably going to meet a horrible death. I got shagged in the nightclub and then killed on the thirteenth floor, naturally. I remember my line as I opened the lift door onto the roof of the car park was, 'Oh no, not the thirteenth floor – just my luck. Fuck . . .' It was obviously important to point this out, just in case anyone watching the film was too stoned on their sofa to read the number on the wall and realize what my ultimate fate was going to be.

I actually loved shooting the death scene best of all. Your adrenalin on set goes through the roof once the cameras start rolling, so you can't feel a thing. You can chuck yourself around much harder than you would in real life and you fall harder – it only hurts much later! They employed a stunt double for me, who had a much more athletic body than I did, but didn't look like me, so I had to get a full prosthetic face mask done. They give you a straw to breathe through and cover your face in clay and then wait for it to set; it was one of the most claustrophobic things I have ever done. It was also very creepy seeing a corpse with your own face on it.

Apart from learning to die and have sex on camera, *Ripper* taught me one other thing. If you go to Hollywood, more often than not you end up in Vancouver. Vancouver is where the tax breaks are; Vancouver is where a huge number of studios shoot their films; Vancouver is where Hollywood goes to work.

I had also been working at MTV for a few months, licking my wounds post *The Big Breakfast*. It was a nice below-the-radar sort of job, and MTV was relatively 'happening' at the time. Richard Blackwood, June Sarpong, Cat Deeley, Edith Bowman and Russell Brand were all working there, and we used to see each other in the make-up rooms and hang out a bit. The offices were in Camden. I did five days a week, and people would ring in to request videos. I was just your average VJ. It was a respectable job, it wasn't glamour, and the pressure was off me. It was a young person's cable channel and no hugely sharp, smart banter was expected of me. I did not have the pressure of people looking at me critically every day, analysing my skirt length or questioning my intellect, or my ability to pronounce three-syllable words. Let's just say words like 'intrepid' didn't come up much! Instead, I could learn my craft a bit more. I stepped out of the whole press thing for a while. I did a couple of glamour shoots, but I'd been really burned by *The Big Breakfast*, so I just wanted to hide.

Weirdly, I was still interviewing the same people I'd been chatting to on the bed at *The Big Breakfast* – Eminem, Britney Spears, Jessica Simpson. It was quite entertaining to see the PR sausage machine in progress. I'd interview one pop band, then they would break up, and six weeks later two members of the band would return with newly fixed-up hair, a couple more piercings, a tattoo and another two blokes in a new band! And I'd be talking to them and saying to myself, I'm sure I've spoken to you before. You look familiar! There was clearly a lot of repackaging going on.

Something *I* wasn't immune to either! I was determined to get my acting career off the ground. I'd also had a small role in a Brit-flick thriller *Sorted*, with Matthew Rhys and Sienna Guillory, but that and my sexy demise in *Ripper* were not quite cutting it. I thought I'd have a better chance of getting work if I signed up to one of the big international agencies. I told Neil Reading over lunch that I wanted to meet with William Morris in order to pursue a film career. I probably shocked him because he said something rude, so I said something rude back, and then I ran out of the Ivy in floods of tears. I very seldom cry and I'm loyal, but I think I knew it was time to move on, although I did miss Faye terribly. It's always hard when professional relationships come to an end. Sometimes they just run their course, or you want a fresh approach, or feel like you need to follow new roads. But you do grow fond of people you talk to on a daily basis. Neil later wrote me a letter apologizing after his outburst in the Ivy, but I was very hurt. I was sick of being told no. I just wanted support and to go for it. Although we haven't worked together since, I still bump into him from time to time and we are always nice to each other. He is doing very well and I'm happy for him.

Then, at the end of 2000, my new agents, William Morris, put me up for a part in a play called *Eye Contact*, written by Neil Monaghan and directed by Izzy Mant. It was a drama about the sexual politics at a lap-dancing club and the unfolding relationships between the punters and the dancers. I was excited to get the part and I didn't mind that I was playing a lap dancer; it was the lead, on stage. It was at the august and revered Riverside Studios in Hammersmith.

I suspect the producer was not that keen on me in the beginning, but after the creators of the show realized how much press coverage they'd get and how many bums on seats the idea of me scantily clad and spinning round a pole would provide, they were thrilled. The play sold out, after we'd placed some staged topless pole-dancing shots in the press. This was a ruse to stop any fearless paps from sneaking in on the opening night and grabbing some shots. The run was also, eventually, extended.

The actual pole-dancing section, for which I trained at the Astral Club in Soho (it was much harder than it looked and I'd come home covered in bruises with strains in muscles I never knew I had), didn't appear in the play until the middle of the second half. I'd spin round the pole and flash a modicum of boob and a tiny bit of bikini-covered arse; the whole scene lasted for about three seconds at most and it would be swiftly followed by a loud groan from the audience: 'Urgh! Is that it?' All these poor blokes had booked themselves a ticket and forced themselves to sit through nearly two hours of theatre in the hope of some tit and titillation; I felt a bit sorry for them. We used to howl with laughter about it after each performance in the dressing room, the thought that we were bringing 'culture' to a whole new audience.

I loved doing that play and made a lifelong friend during it. Preeya Kalidas and I were both from stage school. She went to Sylvia Young, while all the others in the play were from RADA or 'proper' acting school. It was hilarious. You could really see the difference between us even at the warm-up stage. They'd all be going through their vocal exercises, saying, 'Ma-ma-ma-maa-ah. La-la-la-la-lah. Blah-blah-blah.' Which, of course, I respected entirely. Whereas Preeya and I would crank up Destiny's Child, throwing shapes in the dressing room to 'Independent Women' and singing really loudly. Preeya has the most amazing singing voice. She now works a lot with Andrew Lloyd Webber and has since appeared in *Bombay Dreams* and played the title character in the BBC's pop opera *Carmen*. (She has also starred in *EastEnders*, *Bend It Like Beckham* and *Bodies*.) We would make a lot of noise, working out dance routines. Eventually, the other girls got right royally irritated and opted to leave our dressing room, saying, 'This is not how we work. The music is distracting.' So we had the room to ourselves. Not that Preeya and I weren't serious; we just loved music and dancing.

So I was swinging round a pole and disappointing a first- and last-time theatre audience of *Loaded* readers when Jason pissed off to Skibo Castle for Madonna and Guy Ritchie's wedding, which frankly could not have taken place at a more inconvenient time of year. I mean, who gets married on 22 December? It's three days before Christmas! It is the busiest time of year. People have stuff to do, presents to get, selection boxes to buy, Advocaat and glacier cherries to source and trees to get down from the loft. *And* the place was a bloody headache to get to. I had to fly to Scotland. Where the hell was Skibo Castle anyway?

Part of the reason for my annoyance was Jason had been invited up to stay at the castle for five days before the rest of the guests arrived. Madonna had invited Gwyneth Paltrow, Stella McCartney and Debi Mazar up the week before, and Guy had invited up his mates, Jason and Jason Flemyng among them. They were all supposed to use the spa, go shooting (or 'banging' as they called it) and ride horses and have a super-grand time together, while all their girlfriends were not invited. Lena Headey and I were on our own in London, while our boyfriends were at Skibo with Madonna, Gwyneth and Stella; we were not pleased to say the least. Our imaginations were running riot. What were our boys doing with those girls? It made for a very uncomfortable and unhappy five days.

121

Not that I had anything against Madonna. She had been very nice to me. The first time I met her, we had dinner at the Ivy, and she introduced herself and said she'd seen me on MTV as her producers had my show on in the studio all the time while they were writing and recording. Guy, Piers and Jason were also there, as well as a couple of her mates. She was at the end of her goth phase at that point, with long black hair. Jason was very excited, but I was so much younger that it all felt a bit grown-up.

Invitations for the wedding were very strict. You were only allowed to bring your partner if you had been together for more than three years. Matthew Vaughn had just met Claudia Schiffer, but she wasn't allowed to go!

So in the five days while Jason, Piers and Guy were 'banging birds' (as Piers later joked in his best man's speech), and Madonna, Gwyneth and co. were being covered in unctions, I was buying all the Christmas presents, hauling the tree out of the loft and slowly discovering my inner Scrooge. Added to that, on the day I was supposed to travel, it was sodding snowing and our flight was delayed.

I remember sitting at the airport in a foul mood when Claudia Winkleman came up and asked if I was going to Madonna's wedding. It was all supposed to be hush-hush, and because I vaguely recognized her, I presumed she must be a journalist and denied all knowledge. She must have thought I was completely stupid when we ended up on the same plane, along with half the wedding party, being diverted to the same poxy airport in the middle of nowhere. We all had to climb into a fleet of Range Rovers in the snow to get to the castle, which was hours away. We stopped off at a Little Chef on the way and I walked in with Jean Paul Gaultier, all dressed up in his designer clobber – his bleach-blond crop, his spray-on leather and his Breton-striped jumper. The place fell silent and everyone did a double take. It was like a scene out of *Prêt-à-Porter* with all these international showbiz types descending on a small town, trying to score a skanky cup of tea as they sucked on a Marlboro Light before they turned up at Madonna's wedding.

We finally got there, and the wedding was that night. It was beautiful: there were candles everywhere, and Donatella Versace had done the flowers. It was very intimate. All the *Lock, Stock* team were there, and Gwyneth and Stella were bridesmaids. There were only about fifty people in the entire reception and it made you feel very privileged and important, despite being excluded from the hunting, shooting and fishing the week before.

Halfway through the evening, we were all sitting at a table, having eaten our smoked salmon and haggis, and drunk a few glasses of champagne. I'd had a gawp at Donatella Versace and Rupert Everett, and marvelled at Stella McCartney's ability to have a full-blown conversation over my head with my boyfriend without even acknowledging I was there. Then Jason said something that was so nasty and out of character I was totally wrong-footed. He and Guy were talking about some music and I said, 'Oh, who's that by?'

Jason turned to Guy and laughed and said, 'Christ! She doesn't even know who that is!'

They both looked at me and laughed again. It was the first time he had ever done anything like that to me and it made me feel really stupid. So I pulled him aside and said, 'That was not very nice or kind. I think we should go upstairs and have a chat.'

We went to our room and had one hell of a massive row. We were staying in the actual castle, and as I had only just arrived, I had no idea where I was. So when Jason stormed out of the room, I had to follow him, otherwise I wouldn't have been able to get back to the party. He didn't know I was following him, of course, and as he walked down a long corridor, he saw Gwyneth at the other end, walking towards him. When he approached her, Jason started to swing his hips from side to side and do a little jive with his arms.

'Gwynnie . . . Gwynnie . . . Gwynnie . . . Sexy, sexy, sexy!' he exclaimed.

'Hey! Jase!' she said in her transatlantic twang.

Suddenly, she spotted me coming up behind and he realized she'd clocked someone. He turned round, only to be met with my fist in his face!

Gwyneth screamed, 'Oh my God!' – this time sounding way more American – and grabbed her cheeks like something out of that Munch painting. She was so shocked she snatched Rupert Everett's arm – he was just behind her – and together they scuttled off. It was less than dignified. Fortunately, Jason and I worked it out in the end.

I think the fact that Jason had been at Skibo 'banging birds', going on romantic picnics and riding horses had put the wind up us both. Gwyneth did end up briefly dating Alex de Rakoff, who'd been there for the week, so my fears weren't totally unfounded I guess. But any of those girls could have had any one of the men. When they want something, they go for it. I was twenty-one; I didn't stand a chance against a twenty-eight-year-old Oscar-winning movie star. I had a feeling something would happen that week and I was just hoping it wasn't going to be Jason. I have never hit him before or since, but that evening I gave him a massive right hook!

Apart from that, it was a great night.

Madonna and I were on the dance floor together. She has so much energy. She is a wonderful lady, phenomenal. I did see quite a bit of her for a period. I remember having to go and buy her a birthday present and having no idea what to get her. So I bought her a Tocca candle and some frangipani body cream from Fred Segal. She very sweetly sent me an email the next day saying thank you! I thought she was a very genuine person.

Jason and I had turned up at her birthday party in Beverly Hills with the Tocca candle not realizing it was fancy dress. When we arrived, she said, 'You've got to dress Japanese!' Demi Moore looked on sympathetically, dressed as a geisha, as Madonna dragged me up to her bedroom and made me try on her clothes. I ended up borrowing a little Japanese dress and some Céline heels. I remember being very happy that I could fit into her clothes because she is so tiny!

We were quite often invited over for macrobiotic dinner parties, because she and Gwyneth were very big on the whole macrobiotic thing. There were always interesting people there. After he got married to Madonna, Guy kept up with his old friends. However, I do remember Guy getting a personal assistant, and when the assistant called us, Jason would call back asking Guy if his fingers had dropped off. Was he ill? Could he no longer use the phone himself? I think Jason saw it as his duty to keep Guy grounded like that, but at the same time I suspect there was a little part of Jason that had always wanted that himself. Like most sportsmen, he was competitive; he wanted the big house, the PA, the supermodel girlfriend and the Boffi kitchen. And now he has it all.

When I first met Jason, he was a breath of fresh air. He was sporty and healthy and would never drink at home. It was the first time I had met anyone like that. His mum was a health and organic freak. She once gave me a book called *Fit for Life*, which was a revelation. I had never seen or read anything like it. Where I came from I used to know it was suppertime because the chip pan would go on. We'd have fish fingers and chips; beans and chips; pancakes, beans and chips. I remember coming home once from Italia Conti and saying to my mum that I wanted to eat more healthily. I was getting a bit chubby and was also exhausted. I had no energy because I wasn't eating properly. She thought I was being a right pain in the arse. 'Kelly needs white fish and broccoli.' 'Kelly needs fruit.' She did get it for me in the end, but she always thought I was a bit high maintenance.

Apart from the clean living and the organic produce, Jason also introduced me to the joys of Sydenham. Personally, I had wanted to buy a flat in Notting Hill. It was before the film, the blue door and Julia Roberts, and I thought it was a glorious place, full of bohemian shops and cafes, but Jason thought it was poncey and wanted to live near his mates. So we bought a three-bedroom maisonette in Sydenham. I spent the summer doing it up, buying curtains. I remember showing off in a *Sunday*

Times interview, saying I'd moved to South London and I really thought I'd made it: I lived in London! Even though it was South London, it was still London. In reality, I'd left Kent and got as far as Lewisham.

No one was more pleased than my mum when we bought the flat. Almost as soon as I walked down the path with my two black bin liners containing all that I owned, she turned my bedroom into a second bathroom. I could not have moved back home if I'd wanted to! All we had growing up was a tiny shower room; we never had a bath or anything. So as soon as I left, she took over my room. Most people cling on to their children, terrified of empty-nest syndrome, but my mum was the opposite. She couldn't wait to run a hot bath and crack open the Radox.

Jason and I really clicked, and although we were hanging with a late-night party crowd, he protected me hugely from all that. He liked to party, but he never involved me. We were from similar working-class backgrounds and our families became extremely close. But most importantly, I think, both our success stories began at the same time. We were best friends.

I remember in the Easter holidays, back when I was on *The Big Breakfast,* I paid to fly us both first class to the Maldives for a holiday. I booked about four villas at the Banyan Tree for ultimate privacy. I have no idea what I was thinking! It was the first time I really had money and we were both so knackered. It was the best holiday ever. It was the first time either of us had stayed anywhere like that. It was the first time either of us had seen water like that. It was the first time we'd walked on sand like that. Or flown first class. We had a butler. That was what was so lovely about our relationship – it was the first taste of the high life for both of us. To share that with someone you love is amazing. We used to find the same things ridiculous, the same things extraordinary; to sit next to Julia Roberts at the Golden Globes was a silly thrill for both of us. But for me, it was so much more fun when we both had nothing!

And that's how we arrived in LA, with nothing, off the back of the success of *Lock, Stock* and *Snatch*, which was also directed by Guy Ritchie and starred Brad Pitt and Benicio del Toro as well as Jason, Vinnie Jones and Jason Flemyng. I wore a very revealing pink knicker-flashing Julien Macdonald dress to the UK premiere of *Snatch*, having changed in the car! A few months later, in January 2001, we all flew to LA for the premiere there and stayed at the Four Seasons. Vinnie filled his boots at the gift shop in the Four Seasons because it was all going on the film company's bill, as agreed. So he was pulling out boxes of cigars and presents for his family! It was hilarious.

Jason had been invited to meet with various important studio executives, and I was desperate for a change from MTV and the flat in Sydenham, so I resigned and got on the first plane out there with him. Fabulously, we stayed in Vinnie Jones's rented house in the Hollywood Hills, while he was away making a film.

The first thing I noticed about LA was that nearly everyone was unemployed. It is a pyjama town. Everyone is waiting for something to happen, so they go to yoga while they're waiting, or walk around with a Starbucks in their hand while they are waiting. It is not a very sophisticated city, but people do go there to be creative, to do things and better themselves, which I like. It is also a town where things can come out of the blue.

I had one telephone number when I arrived: manager Joan Hyler's. Tim Curry, who is perhaps best known as Dr Frank-N-Furter in *The Rocky Horror Picture Show*, had given it to me on set while we were shooting *Sorted*. She was a very powerful player in LA – she was managing Portia de Rossi and Eric McCormack from *Will & Grace* – and amazingly she took my call. Within three weeks of meeting her she'd secured me a starring role in a sitcom called *The (Mis)Adventures of Fiona Plum* for Warner Brothers.

It was one of those lucky breaks that I never expected would happen to me. The original lead for the show had dropped out at the last minute and somehow Joan had managed to get my foot in the door. It was a sitcom about a British witch who'd been sent to America to look after three children as their nanny – a sort of *Mary Poppins* meets *Bewitched*. I auditioned and Jonathan Prince, the writer, declared out of the blue that he only wanted me for the role. I couldn't believe it. Normally, auditioning and pilot season is such a long and protracted lottery. It is exhausting, and you are up against every Kelly Brook glamour girl from all over the world who thinks she can make it in Hollywood. The process usually starts in January, when they offer all the TV scripts out to the A-list actors like Meryl Streep, hoping that this is the year Meryl will do TV, but once the A-listers have rejected their overtures, the rest of us get a look-in.

There are hundreds of scripts for shows waiting to be cast and you have no idea what is going to be picked up or what will work. Often you can end up backing the wrong horse and you shoot a pilot that just gets canned. It is a long, boring process of auditions with casting directors, directors, producers, then the network. The final hurdle is the network test, but before you can go in, your agent has to do the deal. Your agent and your lawyer will be on the phone to the network doing the deal, negotiating the pilot and your salary per episode, agreeing what you get if and when it goes to series. You know – if you get this job, this is what you will earn. They are doing all this while you're in character in the corridor waiting to go into the room. Quite often the studio makes you sign a six-year contract *before* the audition. They take all the power away from the agent, so you're in no position to negotiate after the network has given you the job.

Fortunately, it was first time lucky and on this occasion English was what they wanted. Plus Michael York was to play my dad, which I thought was genius, as he is so goddam posh! I hired an acting coach, the fantastically talented Belita Moreno, who, as well as being a brilliant actress in her own right, coached the likes of Kate Hudson for *Almost Famous*, for which Kate received an Oscar nomination.

Learning the art of sitcom was incredibly technical; there is a different tone and energy from, say, the theatre. Belita worked with me for hours on the script; she taught me how to be funny; she taught me the difference between walking while delivering a punchline and standing still to deliver it, which was the difference between someone laughing or not. As they say, comedy is all about timing. We worked meticulously not only to find the character and the beats, but also to make it the funniest it could be. I loved doing it, and I got it pretty quickly – it was like learning a dance routine, and I'd had plenty of practice at those.

We filmed on the Universal lot, which was all my childhood fantasies writ large: the big security gates, the giant sound stages, the streets named after Hollywood stars. I couldn't believe I was there. It was August 2001, they'd planned thirteen episodes of the show and we were ready to film. BNC, my publicists, sent me to New York to meet all the magazine editors. I was twenty-one; it was everything I'd ever wanted. And then the studio head, who'd given the green light to the show, left, and the new person who came in didn't like the show. By October they'd cancelled it! I couldn't believe it. I was heartbroken. It was hideous – a massive slap in the face.

Amazingly, my manager, Joan, said that it wasn't good enough, that I needed to be on TV. She badgered them: 'You need to find her a show!' Warner Brothers wanted to put me under exclusive contract, but Joan said no. In retrospect, that may have been a mistake, but she wanted to see if there was a better option. She wanted to keep me non-exclusive. Everyone kept on saying, 'You're great at comedy. You're the next Julia Roberts!' I didn't believe them at all, but I suppose these Hollywood types have to get themselves excited somehow! Everyone wants to discover someone and make them a star. I also had a good story: I was a glamour model who'd done a big TV show, and I was young and full of hope!

Eventually, they wrote me into *Smallville* as Lex Luthor's girlfriend. The series was hugely popular, eventually running for 133 episodes and winning 2 Emmys, and starred Terence Stamp and Christopher Reeve. Back

I went, inevitably, to Vancouver! I was miserable. Jason was in LA, and I was stuck in a Canadian winter freezing my cheeks off. The cast were working non-stop, so there was no one to hang out with. I did four episodes. The whole cast were put on the cover of *Rolling Stone*, and there was a section all about me on the inside. My team did the best they could out of a bad situation. Joan really did pull a rabbit out of a hat. She was extremely impressive. My situation was not uncommon, but it was not the most auspicious of starts.

Meanwhile, Jason and I had just bought a house in West Hollywood and filled it with fabulous 1950s post-modern furniture from garage sales. I remember him coming home with a little chandelier and a wicker rocker for about $50 from down the road. We were like a couple of chavs in Hollywood – I was in Juicy track-suits, stonewashed jeans and a scrunchie, and he wore the same jogging bottoms for weeks at a time. I used to throw away his nasty flip-flops and he'd insist on taking them out of the bin! We were very happy.

Jason got a part in *The Italian Job*, filming in Venice and the Dolomites with Ed Norton, Donald Sutherland and Mark Wahlberg, and I went along as his 'trailer bitch', as Gwyneth used to call those girls who sleep in the hotel, hang around on set and tuck into hot dogs stolen from the craft service (film catering) while watch-ing DVDs all day. Actually, being a trailer bitch on *The*

Italian Job was a bit more enjoyable than on other sets. For a start, the locations were stunning, and also the cast and crew were amazing. Ed Norton was extremely entertaining, and Donald Sutherland was as cantankerous as one would expect. Jason used to chain-smoke all the time, even though Donald had a very strict 'no smoking on set' rule. It would drive Donald nuts every time Jason walked past in a guff of smoke.

The movie was wrapped and we were already back in London when the producers decided they wanted to round up the characters with a little vignette at the end, so they called me and asked if I wanted to play the part of Lyle's girlfriend. (Lyle was played by Seth Green.) I didn't want to step on Jason's toes – it was his big film – but he was sweet and insisted I should accept. So we both flew back to LA and I had a fitting at Paramount. I remember I'd driven around the studios with Jason a year earlier looking at the lots and dreaming of working there one day, and there I was!

By now, I was starting to get offered more parts, and Jason and I were travelling a lot, mostly not together. I went to Mexico, France and Italy, but one of the most memorable experiences was Romania, where I filmed the part of Lea in *House of 9* with Dennis Hopper and Peter Capaldi.

I think we could all tell it was never destined to be a great film but Dennis Hopper didn't care. He adored

Romania and had been there many times before. He knew exactly where to go and what to do. He was a fantastic photographer and took photos of all the night-life and the prostitutes, and even published a book afterwards, *Bucharest Nights*.

Dennis was a great character. He was also a notorious line-stealer, so when we'd improvised scenes the day before, he'd come back the following day and deliver all your lines. He was shameless, but it was Dennis Hopper, so what did I care! Obviously, *House of 9* was another slasher B-movie and Dennis would complain because the screaming girls were dressed in jeans, which was use-less for an exploitation movie: we should have been in skirts. We would all call him an old sexist, but he was right! He was wild and great fun. He took me to the most insane techno club I have ever been to.

The Romanian film studio itself was phenomenal, and the make-up artist was the best I have ever had. When we left, he gave me the most beautiful oil paint-ing. The only really great drawback was the food. It was the same every day: plastic containers of some type of meat, probably pony, vinegary carrots and potatoes. We found a McDonald's, which was a twenty-minute drive from the set and which we'd go to every lunchtime. Eventually, we found a restaurant that had fabulous food – it was so delicious – but Dennis mentioned this place was run by a couple of Italian fascists who would

On holiday in Fiji with Jason Statham. I adored him – he was talented and fun.

Presenting *The Big Breakfast* with Johnny Vaughan in February 1999.
The producers had decided on a strict no-cleavage policy for me!

On the beach being made-up by Ginny Bogado, for *GQ* Woman of the Year 1999. I won!

LEFT: Backstage with Jason, on the opening night of *Eye Contact* – also my twenty-first birthday.

With Jason at the BAFTA awards, both of us embarrassed by the attention. We had no idea how to pose on the red carpet.

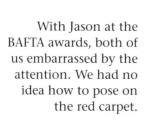

Holding my corpse-face on the set of *Ripper*, my first horror film.

With a couple of the stars of *Smallville*, Tom Welling (aka Clark Kent) and Michael Rosenbaum (aka Lex Luthor).

On the phone to my agent, so exhausted by pilot season in LA that I couldn't get out of bed. He'd just sent me pizza.

Dancing with Jason at
Vinnie Jones's fancy dress
birthday party in January 2003.

A day off in Rome,
when shooting
School for Seduction.

My dad and Jason in Beverly Hills. My parents loved Jason.

With Juan Pablo Di Pace on the set of *Survival Island* (later called *Three*).

And with Billy Zane, my husband on set, who wanted to marry me in real life.

Kissing Billy on the Greek kayiki that he'd learned to sail. We'd hop from beach to beach, restaurant to restaurant.

Filming *Love Island* on Fiji with Patrick Kielty, who was sharp, witty and great company.

With Lisa on the beach in Malibu.

With Emma Pierson on the set of *Hotel Babylon*.

Agatha Christie's Marple allowed me to speak posh, do some acting and keep my clothes on! I loved it. Here with the illustrious Geraldine McEwan and Harry Enfield.

Sailing off St Barts with Billy,
on my twenty-sixth birthday.

With Billy at the Cannes Film
Festival. By now I was used to
posing on red carpets.

Billy's fortieth birthday party ended with a
lot of custard pies being thrown.

A shot from my 2015 calendar – I've done a calendar a year since 2001.

not let Romanians into the restaurant. It was not right, it was offensive and awful, but the food really was amazing, so we'd sit there and eat vegetables from the garden, and homemade pasta, and tiramisu that wobbled like a fat baby's arm, all the while surrounded by fascist paraphernalia that we just blanked because we were so hungry.

We used to discuss it beforehand: 'We'll eat and run. Don't look, don't engage, keep your eyes closed, get the food down as quickly as you can and run for it.' I do honestly think about that food still; it was extraordinary. It was the highlight of the day. The rest of it was grim. We'd all only signed up because Dennis Hopper had signed, and he'd only done that so he could photograph Romanian prostitutes in his bedroom. The tiramisu was the only thing that got us through.

My next film, *School for Seduction*, was written and directed by Sue Heel. It also starred Dervla Kirwan, Margi Clarke and Emily Woof. It was such a good story, about an Italian temptress called Sophia who travels to Newcastle-upon-Tyne to teach a group of Geordies the art of romance, and was based on Sue's life. It was shot in Rome and Newcastle, and was hard work. I think Sue was under immense pressure at the time as she kept breaking down during filming. I didn't know if it was because I was terrible, or because I was marvellous, or because she was stressed. You didn't know the reasons.

She was angry sometimes and I found her very difficult. It was *my* job to be the up-and-down, volatile actress!

It was the first time I had been the star of a film and I soon learned about the amount of shit that gets flung around when you are in that position. It was amazing. The things I heard afterwards were extraordinary. For example: 'We're not going to have a wrap party because Kelly doesn't want one.' I wasn't aware of it. I chose to isolate myself from the rest of the cast because my character in the story was not supposed to be part of their gang, so I think there were a few choices I made that might have been misunderstood. Would I make the same choices again? Probably. I wanted to do the best job possible.

One thing I wasn't doing a very good job of, though, was my relationship with Jason. We were still travelling a lot and not seeing each other very much. Then one day when we were in Malibu together, I thought I might be pregnant. I wasn't, but it made me realize that I did want to have a baby. Jason and I had never talked about having children so I didn't know how he'd react to the idea – I just assumed he'd be on the same page as me. We had a three-bedroom maisonette in Sydenham and were both working and I think we could have afforded it, though obviously it would have meant big changes in our lives. But when I brought it up, it became clear that in his mind he was nurturing a completely different dream. He wanted to focus on becoming an action movie star. I didn't really see why we couldn't do both. We were living together, we were being flown from everywhere to LA and back, and he was on everyone's radar – he was doing well. Would it have held him back? I don't know but while he had every right not to feel ready, I also felt he was not listening to what I needed.

I didn't really see it clearly at the time, but although on the surface Jason and I were doing great – we were making films, we were buying houses – we were not developing as a couple. I was with him for seven years and during that time there was no sign of him asking me to marry him. We were never engaged. And I now realized there would be no children in our immediate future at least. I had been Jason's trailer bitch, given up my career and family in the UK to follow him to the US. And now it seemed as if my dreams no longer came into it. I felt like I had been taken for granted, but I was still very loyal.

So on 24 February 2004, when Billy Zane burst into my life, tripping over and falling flat on his face in the Chateau Marmont clutching a beautiful vine of jasmine that he'd ripped off the plant as he'd passed it, any thought of an affair didn't even cross my mind. I did think he was beautiful. Both my mum and I had been in love with him ever since watching him in *Dead Calm*, when we had both decided he was one of the most handsome men we had ever seen. Understandably, I had been nervous when my agent, Andrew Ruff at Paradigm, had suggested a meeting with Billy. He represented us both and said that Billy had a project that he was keen to talk to me about. And when Billy walked through the door on his thirty-ninth birthday wearing a flat cap and carrying jasmine, I was intrigued. He was beautiful, very charismatic and tall. But it was not love at first sight that afternoon in the Chateau Marmont.

Billy sat down, handed me the jasmine and, as we ordered tea, he gabbled ten to the dozen about the film, *Survival Island* (also known as *Three*), and the part, and I remember thinking, He is the craziest person I have ever met. I'd read the script and I thought I was way too young to play Billy Zane's wife: I was twenty-four at the time. But the way he spoke, the words he used, he was so charming and passionate. He talked a lot of nonsense most of the time, but he could take you on amazing journeys with his tangents and his vivid imagination. He was like no one I had ever met before.

I remember coming home and telling Jason I had met Billy Zane and that he was insane, but that I thought I might screen-test for the role of his wife. Jason wasn't really listening, but he said he was pleased for me.

Less than six weeks later, after passing an audition

too, I was flying to the Bahamas. I was about to stay in a beautiful hotel for three months on a pink sandy beach with lapping turquoise waves, and I was grinning from ear to ear.

I had no idea how my life was going to change. No idea at all.

6

'Have You Met Billy Zane? He's a Cool Dude' (*Zoolander*)

I didn't stand a chance. Or actually, more precisely, my relationship with Jason didn't stand a chance. When Billy Zane wants something, he usually gets it. He is possibly one of the most charismatic, determined people I have ever met; nothing stands in his way. And back in February 2004, he'd decided he wanted me to co-star with him in *Survival Island*, he wanted me to be his wife, and he wanted me to live with him. He just wanted me full stop. Money was no object.

Somewhat unsurprisingly, I got the part of his wife, Jennifer, in *Survival Island*. I then went back to London, to my three-bedroom flat in Sydenham, while Andrew, my agent, negotiated the deal. A few days later, Andrew called and said the producers of the film could not afford to pay me the normal rate that I was getting per film at that stage. I wasn't particularly fussed – I quite fancied doing the film, but I wasn't desperate and I knew I couldn't do it for what they were offering. It really wasn't worth my while. So I politely declined. They called back.

'Billy only wants you to do it, and he is prepared to take a pay cut so you can. He will use his fee on you.'

This is not as unusual as it sounds. Apparently Sharon Stone organized for something similar with Leonardo DiCaprio once, when filming *The Quick and the Dead*. Not that I am comparing myself to him! But I thought it a little odd, as evidently did my agent, who took me out to lunch and asked me if anything was going on. If Billy had a crush on me or anything like that. I remember saying he had been nothing but professional in the audition. I'd worked with him for an hour; he'd put me on tape for the director, told me I reminded him of Julia Roberts and left! I had not sensed anything at all. That shows how switched on my radar was at the time!

Having accepted Billy's generous offer to pay my wages, I flew to Eleuthera with Sadie, an English girl I'd met at a barbecue in LA who became a close friend. Sometimes she would come with me on jobs and help me read scripts and learn my lines. She didn't work for me full-time, but it can be lonely on location so she used to come and stay with me; in return I would pay for the flights and her accommodation. She was keen to become a writer and used to spend her days tapping away on her laptop and her nights hanging out with me.

This was the dream job. We stayed at Cocodimama, a gorgeous little pale blue clapboard boutique hotel on a pristine beach in its own private bay. There was a small lead cast – just Billy Zane, Juan Pablo Di Pace, a handsome young Argentinian actor, and me. Billy was renting a fisherman's house in the town, as we spent all day filming on the beach, but Sadie, Juan Pablo and I were in the hotel, and we were, quite frankly, a lot younger than him, so we were always out swimming and kayaking and didn't really have much to do with him. Billy kept inviting us to dinner almost every night and we kept refusing to go because we'd spent all day together and were too tired from filming. Then one evening, instead of taking no for an answer, he turned up at my room while Sadie and I were watching a film with a large platter of lobster and steak. Billy's a man who'd never do anything low key or banal. He'd gone to town and bought the biggest lobsters he could find, had them cooked and brought them over. It was very sweet but also a little overwhelming.

He loved a big gesture and the first weekend of the shoot he announced that he was taking Sadie and me to Harbour Island. He hired a driver to take us there. We ate in the best restaurants and had the most fabulous time. Billy had an amazing ability to make any place the greatest it could be. I suppose it was because he was older, but he knew the best places to go, the best places for whisky, the best place to eat, the best beach, the best cove, because he had been round the world a hundred times and had done it all with a million different models. He knew the drill; he had a good game. It was intoxicating. I'd travelled the world a bit already, but Billy had a fine aesthetic and a razor-sharp eye for detail. He was a seasoned cad, and I was his new muse.

Two weeks into the shoot, Sadie returned home, leaving me on my own. Jason never visited me on set: he was filming in Canada, and when he did have some time off, he went skiing in Whistler with his manager, Steve Chasman, instead. It was before people really used mobiles, so he'd call my hotel once a day and hope to catch me, and that would be that. It is hard to maintain a relationship with that amount of distance. We were not in contact very much at all during that time.

This suited Billy down to the ground. With Sadie away and Jason out of the picture, he really set out to seduce me.

Inevitably, I ended up falling for him. The dynamic of the film was that I was Billy's wife and I had an affair with Juan Pablo. I was in a love triangle. It was life imitating art. There were lots of kissing scenes with Juan Pablo, which I think drove Billy mad, and when the paparazzi came and took photos of Juan Pablo and me in the water, Billy was not involved in the pictures. He wasn't papped, which I think annoyed him too.

I was in awe of Billy. I have never felt he was the love of my life, but I do feel that our affair was something I needed. It was the first time after all those years with Jason I had been with someone else. It wasn't something I wanted long term. It was definitely supposed to be a fling. I wanted to work things out with Jason. There was clearly something wrong with our relationship, but what I wanted, ultimately, was for us to work.

Billy was very different, not working class like Jason and myself. His parents were semi-professional actors who ran a medical training school in Chicago, and Billy was well travelled and cultured. He was a great lover. He knew what he was doing. I had a wonderful time. I was in the Bahamas; it was sexy, hot and humid. He had the gorgeous fisherman's house in the town; I was living on the beach. It was a fantasy scenario. He wore a check shirt and drove a truck around. He'd pick me up. We'd swim in the sea. It was heaven. I was in a film. He was a movie star I'd always had a crush on. It was the best six weeks of my life. But it wasn't real. It was a 'location-ship'. It wasn't my life.

I came back to London with no interest in seeing Billy again. I knew he hoped otherwise, but I was deter-mined to try and make it work with Jason, although when we saw each other again, it was weird. We were not at all romantic. From the moment I was intimate with Billy I never slept with Jason again. I did feel terribly guilty, and I was also very confused. I didn't know what I felt, or what I wanted. Jason was being cold and I was cold in return.

A few weeks later, Jason and I were asked to present an award at the MTV Movie Awards in LA. So we flew out together and stayed at our house in Hollywood. We went to the after-party at the Chateau Marmont, and Billy knew I was going to be there, as we'd spoken a few times on the phone, and he turned up at the party. In fact, Billy was the first person I saw as I walked in. I thought, Why is he here? This is *so* awkward. But he had made up his mind he wanted me to be his wife, and what Billy wants . . .

I agreed to meet up with him the next day for tea at the Chateau Marmont, where he said he wanted to be with me. I kept on saying, 'What about Jason? I want to be with him. We had a fling, nothing more. And anyway, none of this matters; I'm going back to London tomorrow. Jason is going to Miami to do a film. So that's it.'

The next day, I arrived at the airport, having said goodbye to Jason, to find Billy standing at the gate.

'I'm on your flight back to London,' he announced.

He clearly wasn't going to take no for an answer. We flew to London together in adjacent seats and I remember feeling rather scared and suffocated by the whole thing. I travelled back to my flat in Sydenham, and fortunately he stayed in the Charlotte Street Hotel.

But the very next day, he called and said he'd booked for us to go on holiday together in Greece. A friend of his had rented the *Talitha G.*, Jean Paul Getty's beautiful super-yacht, and Billy wanted to take me on it and sail around the Greek Islands all summer long.

I was in Sydenham; my boyfriend was in Miami, on set, barely returning my calls. I was on a massive comedown. I'd been in the Bahamas, had this fabulous love affair, and now I was back in South London, completely miserable. I was hugely confused to say the least. That afternoon, Billy turned up outside my flat with his chauffeur Alan (who is now my chauffeur and has been for years). We drove around London, talking in the car. He went on about Greece, on about sailing around the Greek Islands, and all I could think was, I can't go. I am still with Jason. I don't know what I am doing, I don't know if I want this.

I asked Billy to drop me off at my dentist on Harley Street but he insisted on waiting in the car for me. I didn't argue, I just jumped out, ran in the front door and straight out the back. I leaped into a taxi and asked the driver to take me to Brighton. I disappeared.

In fact, I went to Sadie's house. I turned up on her doorstep and told her I had run away.

'I can't do this. I can't go to Greece with Billy,' I said.

'I don't know what I want. I need to speak to Jason. He's my priority. I love him. I need to sort things out with him. I have got myself into a situation I can't get out of.'

Billy was furious. To this day, I still have no idea how long he sat outside the dentist before he realized I was never coming out. He started calling everyone, trying to find out where the hell I was.

Finally, I managed to speak to Jason and I told him about the affair. I was sobbing as I said I was sorry, that I wanted to be with him and to go to Miami to work things out. I asked if I could go and talk to him. He wouldn't let me and I ended up begging. 'I'll just come and make smoothies. I'll mix your protein shakes.'

He was so angry with me he didn't want to see me. So I left Brighton and went back to Sydenham and sat there rocking in a corner on my own, wondering what on earth I should do. I had wanted to fly to Miami, to work things out, but now I just couldn't see how to fix things. I was stuck between a rock and a hard place.

Suddenly, there was a knock on the door. I opened it and there was a small Greek man standing there with a box. He told me his name was Marcos.

'This is from Billy,' he said, handing me the box. 'He really wants you to join him in Greece.'

Inside were shells from the beach, a pair of the most beautiful earrings and a letter from Billy declaring his undying love for me. He'd made a collage of pictures of us together in the Bahamas and had written out part of a poem I had given him on the beach in the Bahamas, 'The Invitation' by Oriah.

It was summer, I was stuck in Sydenham, and I was supposed to be dealing with the builders who were doing up the three-bedroom semi-detached house Jason and I had bought together in Dulwich Village. But I was twenty-four years old and I wasn't interested in a three-bed semi in Dulwich. On the one hand, I had Jason, who didn't want to speak to me or see me, and on the other, I had Billy, who was sending me the beach in a box. So I decided to go.

I booked myself an EasyJet ticket to Athens. Billy was waiting for me at the airport, with a helicopter on standby, and we flew to Paros. We went straight to a little bar on the beach, where I got rather drunk, before arriving at the marble mansion belonging to his friend, where I leaped into the pool and then passed out on a sunbed. I was in Greece.

I spent the next ten days as Shirley Valentine, having the most beautiful time. Billy learned to sail a kayiki, an old-fashioned Greek fishing boat, and we'd hop from beach to beach and restaurant to restaurant. Billy loved food and he loved wine. Jason was a former athlete, so I'd spent my life in Californian Vegan, a health food shop, drinking coconut water and eating brown rice. We never went to fancy restaurants, and if we drank alcohol, it was a big night, when he'd get plastered and then atone for it for weeks afterwards. But Billy was an epicure and I loved that. So we ate and drank in the sun for ten days. It was food, wine and sun, exactly what my soul needed. I'll never forget the evening we helped some locals paint the church. We drank some ouzo and watched the sun go down. Afterwards we swept out the church and lit some incense. It was fantastic. I looked like a different person. I felt like a different person. Despite all the food and wine, I lost loads of weight. I looked amazing.

Meanwhile, Jason was calling my mother. My mum was beside herself with anger. She loved Jason and he knew our family well, as we'd been together for so long. She couldn't understand why I would run off with Billy. She told Jason I was in Greece with my girlfriend Lizzy. She told him she'd kill me when I got back. She *loved* Jason, and so did my dad. Our families had had Christmases together. It affects everyone when you break up a relationship that has been going on for so long. My mum and dad were not happy with me. This was not how they'd brought me up. This was not how to treat people. This was not good behaviour. I was not at all popular.

When I got home, I thought, Oh my God, I am back to real life. Which at this point looked really messed up. The whole time I had spent with Billy had been on holiday – six weeks in the Bahamas, then Greece – and now I was back in Sydenham. It was a bit of a slap in the face!

My entire affair with Billy could possibly be seen as one of the biggest mistakes of my life, but then again Jason had made it pretty clear he didn't want children. I had been with him for seven years and there was nowhere for me to go. He didn't want to get married, and he didn't want to have children. What was I supposed to do?

But I still hadn't made my decision to be with Billy. Jason and I had a house in LA, two houses in London; we had a *life* together. It was kind of a marriage and could not be unravelled that easily. We had stuff to deal with regardless of whether or not I was going to be with Billy. When I'd say this to Billy, he'd simply reply, 'It's just logistics.'

I took a small part in *Deuce Bigalow: European Gigolo*, filmed in Amsterdam. It was a great opportunity to work with Rob Schneider, get away and get some sort of head-space. But Billy had other plans. I came back to the hotel one evening after filming and there he was!

He was sitting in the lobby with his great friend the Hitchhiking Poet, Tim O'Connor, who was dressed in a black Stetson and skinny jeans. I had never seen anything like it. Billy told me he was famous for his song 'Knee Beards'. The pair of them were mad. I was slightly embarrassed and hoped no one would see me with these two anomalies! They were very mellow, having spent the whole afternoon sampling the delights of a 'coffee shop', and had got into my room, where Billy had plastered the walls with pictures and cuttings and photos of me. It was like some sort of shrine/crime scene when the murderer's secret 'special' room is finally revealed. I wasn't very impressed; it was all a bit disconcerting. Billy then announced that his friend who'd rented the *Talitha G.* had a house in Saint-Tropez and we'd been invited for the weekend.

So I wrapped in Amsterdam and we flew to Nice. To begin with, we stayed at the Colombe d'Or in Saint-Paul de Vence. A favourite of Picasso, it was stunning and I fell in love with the place. We then hired a car and drove down to the Hôtel du Cap, where we stayed for a few more days.

But there's a problem with the Hôtel du Cap: it's expensive and it only takes cash! There's something about withdrawing a large sum of money from a cash machine that makes you face reality. As I took out the equivalent of £1,000 in crisp notes to pay the bill, I was thinking, I don't really want to be in the Hôtel du Cap. It's not my sort of place, and it is not somewhere I would have chosen. I was more than a little bit pissed off with Billy at that moment. I thought, I shouldn't be doing this. This is not my life. I can't afford to be doing things like this, and even if I could, I wouldn't be stupid enough to be doing them. I should be working. I am at the working stage of my life. I am not living this life yet. Where I come from, you don't buy things you can't afford; you live within your means. The idea of living a champagne lifestyle on lemonade money made me nervous.

We spent the afternoon swimming in Antibes, where all the yachts and boats are moored, and I got a terrible ear infection just as we arrived at Billy's Russian friend's house – a stunning villa on the water in Saint-Tropez, complete with helicopter pad and hot and cold running staff and chefs. A doctor came to the house and told me I wasn't allowed to fly for a week. I'd only wanted to come to the south of France for a weekend; I needed to get back to London. Suddenly, I was stuck in an oligarch's house in Saint-Tropez.

Billy very sweetly suggested we go for a walk around the town to cheer me up, but we were photographed together. It was a nightmare! Photos of me walking around Saint-Tropez eating an ice cream with Billy were splashed all over the papers in the UK. A journalist called up Jason in Miami.

'Kelly's in Saint-Tropez with Billy Zane.'

'Kelly's never been to Saint-Tropez,' he said. 'Kelly's never been to the south of France.'

'Well, we've got photos of her there with Billy Zane.'

Jason called me on my mobile, at which point I
started weeping, telling him how sorry I was, that
I wanted to be with him, that I loved him. He was my
best friend and I couldn't bear the thought of losing
him. I told him I couldn't fly and was in so much pain
from the ear infection but that I'd leave as soon as I
could. I can see that this must have sounded like an
excuse. He hung up on me. That was it. I was honestly
devastated. Devastated, and still stuck in an oligarch's
house in Saint-Tropez with an ear infection and no way
of getting home. What was supposed to have been a
fabulous, glamorous weekend on the Riviera had turned
into a nightmare, and poor Billy was also stuck there,
trying to be kind and bringing me food and little
presents, while I was just totally and utterly miserable.

My life had fallen apart and there was nothing I
could do about it. The irony was that if Jason had said at
any point in all of this, 'Come to Miami. Fly over and
come and see me,' I'd have gone at the drop of a hat.
But the truth was, I had humiliated him and I had done
it publicly. There really was no going back.

So I tried to enjoy the helicopter trips to amazing
little French village restaurants for lunch, or the trips in
the limo for dinner, but my heart was broken and I was
the one who had broken it.

When I finally returned to the UK, I went back to
Sydenham and packed my bags and flew to LA. I went

to the house that Jason and I had bought in West Hollywood, and Billy moved into the Hotel Bel-Air. Wherever I went he'd follow.

A few days later, Billy asked me to the Hotel Bel-Air for dinner and suggested we go for a late-night swim. I said it was a bit cold, but he was insistent. We were splashing around in the oval mosaic swimming pool when Billy suddenly said, 'Stay here.' He sank to the bottom of the pool, got onto his knees, pulled a box from the pocket of his trunks and surfaced with a £60,000 diamond engagement ring from Tiffany wedged between his teeth. It was massive and completely beautiful. He gave it to me and then went back underwater, where he mumbled, in bubbles, 'Will you marry me?'

I was blown away. I was absolutely blown away. We were in this amazing location and Billy had made the most flamboyantly romantic gesture – and when someone asks you that question out of the blue, you only have a split second to decide what your answer is going to be. Everything rushed in on me and I heard myself saying, 'Yes. I will!'

I put the ring on. I was completely stunned.

In the cold light of the following day, all I could think was, I am engaged! I am engaged. How the hell can I be engaged when I am still effectively living with Jason? I looked around my house and I was living with someone else. I had so much I had to deal with.

I couldn't just go and get engaged. I had never met anyone like Billy, but this was ridiculous!

I remember picking Sadie up from the airport and telling her I was engaged. She was so shocked. I think I'd really lost the plot, practically lost my mind. Billy planned for us to get married in Vegas at the weekend and I went and bought some white cowboy boots and a white knee-length broderie anglaise dress from Catherine Malandrino. It wasn't the sort of thing I thought I'd be getting married in. Quite what I thought I was doing with white cowboy boots I don't know, but I didn't even know where to begin. I had never been one of those girls who had imagined what their wedding would be like. I thought maybe this would just be it. Vegas. Cowboy boots. That'll work. It's a shotgun wedding, sort of 'Yeehah!' I really had no idea. At all.

I called my mother and told her I was getting married. She went ballistic on the phone and started shouting, 'What are you going to do? Go to Vegas? And do it at the weekend?' I was slightly taken aback. How did she guess? She then called Billy, who asked her rather sarcastically how exactly she would like us to get married and what exactly she wanted us to wear. She was stunned.

Meanwhile, Billy was booking private jets to take me, Sadie, his friend Todd and his wife, Celine, to Vegas. He'd booked the chapel, the cars, the restaurant, the whole thing. It was all *on*. It was happening. There was no way I could back out.

On the morning of my wedding, I woke up and looked around my house and there were still photos of Jason on the sideboard. All I could think was, I'm getting married today. How am I going to get married?

Sadie turned up to collect me. She was all dressed up. I started to put on my clothes, then sat down on the bed and burst into tears.

'I don't want to go,' I kept saying. 'I don't want to get married. I'm still living with Jason. I still love Jason. I can't do this to Jason. An affair is one thing, but running off and getting married. I love him too much to be so horrible. If Billy really loves me, he'll understand. He's got to understand that this is not happening today. I'd never do that to Jason. It's too cruel.'

I was in my wedding dress with the white boots on, in full make-up. It felt so superficial. Billy and I had never lived together. I knew nothing about his family. We'd both been playing roles in some fantasy film, and suddenly reality hit me and I panicked. I couldn't get married. It was madness. We didn't know anything about each other.

Billy was calling Sadie, trying to find out what was going on: the jet was waiting. Eventually, he realized I wasn't coming. Ever hopeful, he put the jet on standby and drove over to my house. I asked Sadie to let him in.

I didn't know what to do. Finally, she let him in. He was standing there in a gorgeous pale grey suit, with a pink shirt and a matching flower in his lapel. He looked so handsome.

'I can't do this,' I said. 'Can't we just go and have dinner somewhere, all of us? I can't go to Vegas.'

He'd booked the penthouse of the Chateau Marmont for the party in the evening. The idea was that we'd fly to Vegas, get married and come back again for the party. It was all so Hollywood and not me at all. If I was going to get married, I wanted my mum to be there, my nan. I had no idea what I was doing.

In the end, we went to the Chateau Marmont and everyone was very upset. It was terrible. Everyone was very deflated. Billy's friends Todd and Celine were mortified. I think that night Billy had a bit of a breakdown and realized this was not the way to do things and that I had stuff I needed to deal with. If this was ever going to work, he had to slow down to my pace.

I said to him that if I was going to break up with Jason, I needed to do it on my own terms and not because of him, and that I needed to be on my own and not go from one relationship straight into another. I needed some time to think. I wanted to be on my own, live on my own, buy my own house and discover what I liked and figure out what I wanted to do without compromise. I'd spent seven years with someone, buying sofas because he liked them, and I didn't want to do the same thing with someone else. I needed to live my life.

Billy could be quite controlling sometimes and I think he saw me as a project, a blank canvas, his muse. He had an assistant called Jennifer de Rey, and shortly after I met Billy, he sent her to work for me, and the first thing Jennifer was instructed to do by him was to get rid of all my clothes. Much like Kanye West did to Kim Kardashian, so Billy reinvented my wardrobe. I was living in Juicy Couture tracksuits and Ugg boots. I was quite chavvy in my clothes taste and always wore bright colours, and he hated it. He said I should wear gorgeous 1950s clothes and dress in a more feminine way. He knew what would suit me. Growing up, his fantasy was all those Bond girls from *Thunderball* with headbands, knotted shirts and capri pants. He thought I looked like a Bond girl, like Raquel Welch, so he projected that onto me. Jennifer took all my clothes to the charity shop! I remember Sadie coming round and asking where my clothes had gone and I said they'd all been thrown away!

I was also wary about Billy's desire to marry me so quickly. I knew he loved me and wanted to marry me anyway, but I couldn't help wondering from time to time if he had a practical reason for rushing – my British passport. It was just a suspicion and I knew I was probably worrying over nothing so I didn't ask him about it, but I was aware he wanted to work in Europe. A lot of movies were being made in Europe at the time and he was desperate for a European passport. Also, a lot of Hollywood production had been moved up to Vancouver, and for tax reasons, Brits were much easier to employ. Actors like Colin Farrell and Gerry Butler were the new leading men in Hollywood and they were being chosen ahead of the Americans. There was talk of Billy using his grandmother from Sparta to get him a Greek/ EU passport. It was a conversation that was always going on in the background and it was proving tricky. But if he married me, he would instantly be eligible for a UK/EU passport.

So I was determined to get my own show on the road, put a little distance between us and gain some perspective. I bought a tiny little Spanish house on Camrose Drive in the Hollywood Hills, just below the Hollywood Bowl. It was bohemian and completely different from the house I had with Jason. I spent the next year auditioning for films, making the garden pretty and hanging up trinkets. I had my girlfriends visit me and got on with life. Being without Jason made me appreciate how much he did during our relationship, taking on the stress of dealing with builders, always ready to sort out any practical problems. I was glad we'd stayed friends, and by now he had started dating again.

Billy also, eventually, found somewhere to live. In

161

fact, it wasn't until that point I realized he'd had nowhere to live before – he'd been effectively homeless the whole time we'd been swanning around the world living in hotels.

He'd spent a few months in Australia before I met him, and all his stuff was in storage. It was an amazing treasure trove of beautiful furniture, wedding outfits from Morocco, where he made *Cleopatra*, extraordinary stuff, incredible art. He offered me some items for my new house and I said, 'Possibly.' But I turned up one day to find my house completely full of his stuff: his chairs, his masks, all his art. So I told him to take the whole lot out again. It was ridiculous. I don't know what he thought he was doing. Maybe he didn't actually think. Eventually, he used it to fill his rented duplex in Hancock Park, near his sister.

But looking back, I think that was kind of the beginning of the end. He was extremely upset with me. I'd stood him up at the wedding; I didn't want to live with him but I was walking around with this massive engagement ring on, mainly because I felt I wanted to show him some kind of commitment. He wanted me to commit totally to him and I just never would. He was too unpredictable. I didn't trust him 100 per cent. There were all these grand gestures, but his lifestyle seemed to me to be completely unsustainable.

At that point. I'd saved up all my modelling money

and had been really lucky with property. I'd kept the Sydenham maisonette (Jason had kept the Dulwich house) and my properties in London and LA had tripled in value so for someone who had come from nothing, I had set myself up really quite well. I was very independent and successful. I didn't want to marry Billy because I didn't want to find myself in a situation where I'd have to give him half of what I'd worked hard for if another muse came along, the next twenty-four-year-old. I was very aware of all that stuff, which is why I never threw myself 100 per cent into the relationship. Yet in the press I was portrayed as a gold-digger. Apparently, I was only after Billy Zane because he was a movie star and I was a wannabe actress who wanted his money. It wasn't true. I didn't need him for anything.

And he was too impulsive. The first Christmas we spent together, Billy suggested we fly to Australia. I thought, I've pissed off my entire family by splitting up with Jason, so I'll bugger off to Australia. Billy was the only one who wanted to see me. I had a ticket to LA and could do the rest on Air Miles. So I called him up and said, 'Let's do it.' I was relieved I had something to do that didn't involve sitting on my own in Kent.

I went out shopping and bought him a Rolex watch, cufflinks from Dunhill and so on. I spent more than £10,000 on him. I was excited. It was going to be our first Christmas together. I flew to Australia, he turned up at the hotel, and I gave him all his presents; he gave me a T-shirt from Fred Segal. I was stunned and I thought, OK, this git has put no thought into it at all! Then he said his ex-wife, Lisa, lived in Sydney and that he was going to call her and see if he could go and meet her for lunch. I was furious. I said it was so inappropriate, that I didn't fly all the way to Australia just to watch him hook up with his ex-wife! He said it was immature of me to think that. I thought, You cheeky shit. I have left my family at Christmas, and you're planning on spending the day with your ex-wife! In the end, he didn't see her, or at least I think he didn't. Who knows?

We spent three days in Sydney, which were miserable. Christmas, on our own in a hotel; it was nowhere near as much fun as you'd think. It was terrible. We then spent the next week and New Year in Byron Bay, which thankfully was fabulous. I'd never been to Australia before, but Billy, of course, had. He knew exactly where to go, where to eat and what to do. We found ourselves starting to look at houses in Byron Bay. We started looking at macadamia-nut farms, because wherever Billy goes he's always going to buy a house. After viewing macadamia-nut farms in Australia, beach houses in St Barts, ranches in Topanga Canyon, artists' lofts in the south of France and a large rock (they called it an island) in Greece, I plumped on spending my money on a farmhouse in Kent, much to his dismay.

Obviously it wasn't all bad with Billy. I had done living in Beverly Hills with the big fat pool and the big fat car, but with Billy I clicked into a different LA. He'd lived there since he was nineteen, and now he was thirty-nine. He knew it like the back of his hand. He took me to the silent movie theatre to watch Buster Keaton films. I started to watch different types of TV, like *I Love Lucy*, and began absorbing American culture. Billy stimulated me in a way that was entirely new to me. He was very passionate and artistic and creative. He was my tastemaker.

He loved women. That much was obvious, as photographs of him posing with various women adorned the walls of nearly every restaurant we visited. I lost count how many times I fine-dined in full view of snaps of one of his many exes. But he did adore his mum and his sister. We had a very volatile, very passionate relationship. We had a great sex life. There was nothing Billy liked more than making up. I remember once in Camrose Drive we'd had a huge row about something and I was woken up that night by a message on my phone that said, 'Look out of your window.' He'd gone to a garage and bought twenty rosebushes and filled my garden with roses. Then he'd rigged an old record player in the garden and was serenading me with a Tom Waits song to which he was waltzing around. We should all have a Billy in our lives really.

★

It was February 2005 and I had finished *Deuce Bigalow: European Gigolo* and had been doing pilot season in LA, taking meetings, doing auditions, when my UK agent called me about a new TV show that was being developed for ITV. Having been severely burned by *The Big Breakfast*, I was honestly not that keen. But I had been talking to my UK management, who'd kept on telling me it was hugely important to be on TV. The power of the model was waning. The world of high fashion had been flooded by pretty, wan girls from Eastern Europe. Models were beginning to lose out to personalities. It was no longer good enough to be just another pretty face in the increasingly large crowd; you had to have profile, traction, a brand; you had to be someone. Television faces and actresses were getting all the campaigns and magazine covers. Angelina Jolie was the face of St John; Sarah Jessica Parker was advertising Gap; Davina McCall was doing Herbal Essences. Models were just not selling. Even Kate Moss was having a bit of a cocaine blip, having been snapped with a rolled-up tenner on the front page of the *Sun*. (Only to bounce back even higher.) So celebrities were taking over, and just in terms of business if you were not on TV, you were nobody.

Television producer Natalka Znak flew out to LA to meet me. She was working on the hugely successful series *I'm a Celebrity . . . Get Me Out of Here!* and she said she was talking about creating a new show called

Celebrity Love Island. It was a high-concept series and the supposed opposite to *I'm a Celebrity*. At the time, everyone was looking for a televisual Shangri-La, a format they could sell all over the world. TV was no longer presenter-led, or presenter-centric. The presenters were just conduits for the formats. The formats were where the money was.

So the idea was to take ten celebrities and, instead of stripping away all their luxuries, as in *I'm a Celebrity*, *Love Island* would put them in paradise, make it all as glamorous as possible and hope that they hooked up with one another. The programme's developers thought that regardless of the romance, just putting some celebrities together would be fascinating viewing, and if they set them tasks to do, it would be even more entertaining. They wanted them all to be good-looking. Natalka sold it to me as the reality version of *The OC*, with hot people on a beach. So among others they chose Calum Best, Rebecca Loos and Abi Titmus – they wanted sexy young people who'd been in the press a lot; it didn't matter why. The idea was there'd be sex. Loads of sex. Between sexy young people. And the show would be really . . . sexy. And there *was* plenty of sex. Unfortunately, it being an ITV show, it was rather difficult to broadcast it. The crew and I watched loads of racy footage that the public never saw.

I am not sure why I said yes. It was not the most

beguiling or indeed interesting of ideas, and frankly, I wasn't keen to go. The only thing that was remotely alluring was the possibility of spending a couple of months in Fiji. I should really have said no, because as soon as I signed the contract, I began to regret it. In fact, I made the production company's life very unpleasant before I went, in a pathetic, rather juvenile bid to get myself fired before we started. But it didn't work. In the end, they paid me some astronomical fee to go to Fiji for three months. I kept on increasing my demands in the hope that someone would eventually tell me to piss off, but Natalka agreed to everything. I think she was so obsessed with me doing the job that she agreed to it all. I even demanded a producer credit, knowing that would surely be a deal-breaker. They agreed on 'consultant producer' – whatever the hell that means! In the end, I thought, I've got to go. There was no way out of it. I had signed and that was that. But in hindsight, it was not the cleverest way to start a job, because by the time I got there they *all* hated me! And you can hardly blame them: I must have sounded like the most appallingly spoilt, foot-stamping diva.

The one person I really got on well with was Patrick Kielty, who was sharp, witty and just great company. *And* he was good. I hadn't done live TV for years, but he had vast experience from his time as a stand-up. So when the autocue went down and there were acres of dead air to fill, he was the man to stand next to. I was often the brunt of his jokes, but I didn't really care, as he made both of us look good. I liked him very much.

However, shortly after we went on air, the show started to get hammered back home. The critics thought it was terrible, and I think Patrick was really taking all that to heart. I was a little bit more sanguine about it, because I had been through that sort of shit-storm before.

The problem was that the show was boring. Nothing happened. Famous people just hung out on the beach, talking about very little to other slightly less well-known people. I remember making the mistake of telling Patrick that I'd been at school with one of the contestants, Paul Danan, and we'd had a little bit of a bike-shed snog, which Patrick decided to share with everyone back home. I wouldn't have minded so much had Paul not been making a right dick of himself at the time. However, what it did mean was that because I knew Paul, I knew slightly how his mind worked.

Back in the States, I had watched the US version of *I'm a Celebrity* and had seen a girl on the show who was a blonde *Playboy* Playmate called Nikki Ziering and who was very sexy. I mentioned her to Natalka over breakfast one day as the sort of person we needed to spice up *Celebrity Love Island*. There was no chemistry on the show, but as soon as Natalka flew her in, things cranked

169

up no end. Within a day Paul had her up against the wall in the shower. All we saw was steam, and her feet against the glass. It was one of the funniest, most shocking things I have ever witnessed. It was reality-TV gold and just what everyone wanted and the show needed! So perhaps I did deserve my co-producer credit after all!

Celebrity Love Island was a massive production – we took over two Fijian islands and sailed boats to work every day at 4 a.m. Luckily, though, we'd be finished by 9.30 a.m. and would have the rest of the day to ourselves. At the weekends, Billy and I would take helicopters or boats to visit all these beautiful islands: Turtle Island, Matamanoa, Matalele. They were gorgeous five-star honeymoon retreats, which were extraordinary to visit on a weekend. I am not sure I appreciated how lucky I was at the time. Patrick had three girls with him who were part of his team, so he hung out with them, but we did have fun together.

One weekend, Patrick hired a huge catamaran and we all sailed to Tavarua, where Kelly Slater goes surfing, and watched dolphins. It was fabulous. Obviously when you are working, it makes it a little less fabulous, because there are all these work tensions bubbling under the surface, and we knew the show was being gently barbecued back home. But it was hardly a miserable, taxing job chipping away at the coalface of entertainment.

Billy and I did keep ourselves quite separate a lot of

the time. He loved to paint, so he was often off down the beach with his brushes, and we were in our own little bubble. We had only been together about a year and our relationship was still fresh and intense. He was dressing me and making sure my hair and make-up were right, policing my wardrobe for any sniff of Juicy Couture. I think he was at the height of his obsession with me. He would turn up on set every morning and hang around all day; he would not let me out of his sight. He became *my* trailer bitch!

Oddly, when *Love Island* was due to come back on air for a second series, I thought, I don't have any TV on at the moment. I think I quite fancy that again. Three months in Fiji hanging out with the witty Patrick Kielty, what's not to like? But they said no. They didn't want me back! They said I had been a pain in the arse, and frankly, they were right. Fair enough. I wouldn't have employed me again either! They hired the charming Fearne Cotton instead. And who can blame them?

I have to admit, I did have my American agents get involved in a British contract, which I should not have done, as they were on a different page from the UK guys. There was a real gap beginning to open up at the time between the sort of work that I was being offered in the US and that in the UK. In the US, I'd go for an audition, I'd have a screen test, and I'd be at the network the next day. In the UK, I couldn't even get through the door for a sitcom. It is so much more snobby over here. Here, producers have no interest in seeing me as an actress in spite of the work I've done on stage. I think they consider me as a celebrity and way too mainstream. For there is nothing the Brits like more than a box, and woe betide anyone who tries to squeeze out of it, because everyone will try their damnedest to force you back in there. You have to know your place. Some people manage to find their way out, like Vinnie Jones. Before he did *Lock, Stock*, he was just an angry footballer who once grabbed Gazza's bollocks. But he managed to escape; he leaped out of his box and developed a Hollywood film career. It is annoying to be typecast.

So after the slow car-crash that was *Celebrity Love Island*, I headed back to LA with Billy, where honestly, the parts were not coming thick and fast. Fortunately, the advice to get my behind back on the TV had worked and I began to develop a swimwear range for New Look in the UK. I had long ago realized that my true strength lay in diversification, so I have never truly let go of the modelling and my calendars. About half of my income comes from product ranges and endorsements, and my collaboration with New Look has always been one of the most productive and interesting strings to my bow.

New Look is a huge company, with a turnover of £1.48 billion, and sells something like a pair of jeans every 15 seconds in the UK. The brainchild of Tom

Singh, it is all about style, volume and turnover. My first 1950s-inspired swimwear range, which I launched in April 2006, was hugely successful (selling 80 per cent above prediction), and I have since gone on to launch a fashion range (with 4 seasonal drops a year), taking over from Giles Deacon. I have also done a make-up range. I sell about 10,000 nail varnishes a week for New Look at the moment and also help raise their profile in the media. It is a relationship that works, and it is also creatively interesting.

Something I erroneously thought *Fishtales* might be. Andrew Ruff, who managed Billy and me, had at last come through. He had reached the conclusion that Billy and I should do something together, so he came up with a script called *Fishtales*. It sounded intriguing; it was the story of a friendship between a mermaid and a little girl set on a Greek island and was written by Melissa Painter, a single mother from Santa Monica. I took myself off to Palm Springs for the weekend to read it and thought it was fabulous. I immediately went to Santa Monica, had a cup of tea with Melissa and loved her. I took the script to London, gave it to Ron Rotholz, a movie producer I know, and Ron took it to Alki David, the heir to Coca-Cola Hellenic, a shipping and bottling company, who not only has a film production company but also a house on the Greek island of Spetses. Alki loved it, bought it and then walked off with it. Well, both he and

Billy walked off with it. Not that either of them would see it that way, I'm sure. Billy became very heavily involved in the project and I was edged out of the production side, which pissed me off hugely at the time. Alki rewrote the script, he wanted to direct it, produce it, edit it, act in it (he wrote himself in as a baddie), *and* he eventually distributed it. All of a sudden this cute film became something else, not better or worse, just different.

We went to Spetses and stayed in a sweet little white-washed hotel with a cool swimming pool. However, I ended up having a row with the pair of them, calling them both all sorts of names! Alki's vision and my vision were so very different. Perhaps I was much more protective of the original story because I had met Melissa and had really liked her and her concept. The day Alki barked at me that 'This film is going to be bigger than *Harry Potter*' was the day I realized I was wasting my breath. The film went straight to DVD.

Weirdly, one of the projects that really did make me happy and also changed my life, bringing me back to Kent, the place I had perversely spent so many years trying to escape, was *Agatha Christie's Marple* for ITV in 2006. The role of young governess Elsie Holland was an unlikely role for me to get. Having spent all those years at Italia Conti only being put in for the *EastEnders* and *Grange Hill* parts because of my accent, I was now required to speak posh, actually do some acting and keep my clothes on! I was also consorting with some rather illustrious company. Geraldine McEwan, Frances de la Tour, Emilia Fox, Sean Pertwee, Imogen Stubbs, John Sessions, Harry Enfield, Keith Allen and Ken Russell were all in the cast. It was like a *Who's Who* of the country's leading talent. I have to admit I was a little intimidated at the time. Fortunately, I had Ros Simmons, a dialect coach, to help me mind my Ps and Qs, and learn RP (received pronunciation), and I had the most fabulous costumes, courtesy of Frances Tempest, made from Liberty print with small pearls sewn into the nipples for the full 1950s pert-boobed effect. In fact, I loved the costumes so much that at the end I bought the lot as I couldn't bear to be parted from them.

We did some filming in and around Chilham in Kent. Perhaps it was a reaction to the concrete car park architecture of LA or the fact that I had had enough distance from where I'd come from by now – I am not sure – but I fell in love with the Kent countryside, the rolling hills, the medieval villages, the hedgerows, the green fields and the famous blossom trails; turns out I had missed them after all. My parents found a medieval farmhouse that had recently come onto the market. It had an apple and pear orchard, a herb garden and a spring running right the way through it, and the truth was, for better or worse, I really did miss my family. I missed my brother and his son, and my sister and her little boy. I wanted to be near them. I wanted them to have an aunty who was around and in their lives. Also, having the house in Kent meant they could use it – swim in the pool, eat the apples, lie in the sun – even when I was not there.

I snapped up the house. The irony of me buying in Kent didn't pass me by.

7

Titmatized

In the end, the phone call that came in January 2007 about my dad being ill that forced me to go home was perhaps not the great tragedy I thought it was. Perhaps it was my lucky escape. All of a sudden I was back living in Kent with my family and there was something much bigger going on than Billy and me and our 'fairy-tale' life. I just didn't have time for that fancy existence any more. That bubble had burst and reality had come steaming in.

Billy came to live with me in Kent. He did a play in London with Claire Bloom, he was travelling and doing films, but when he wasn't, he was painting at my house in Kent. I can't imagine the light was very good for him, but that's what he did while I spent time with my dad. But Billy was in and out. My parents were never very keen on him. They didn't understand him. They had liked Jason and used to refer to Billy as 'arty-farty'.

I remember Billy going to film in Dallas and all of a sudden thirty Stetsons in boxes were delivered to my door in Kent. He'd gone on a hat-buying rampage and had decided he didn't want just one Stetson; he'd have the whole lot and ship them to me. Another time I was sitting at home and a huge plastic cow arrived covered in daisies; he'd bought it at an auction. My dad mounted it wearing one of the Stetsons. There was never a dull moment.

During the autumn of 2007 I was dividing my time between my father and *Strictly Come Dancing*. There was something about the show that made Billy extremely jealous. I am not sure whether it was the exposure, the fact that I was dancing on television every Saturday night, or whether it was because I was busy and he was not and was stuck in Kent. Or perhaps it was my friendship with Brendan. Whatever it was, it made Billy furious; he couldn't bear it.

My dad passed away in the November and the next few days went by in a blur. I remember feeling oddly euphoric that my father had actually died. I think the dying was worse than the death. I wasn't angry or crying. I think I was probably in shock. I had never really been through a bereavement, and I was worried the freight train was going to hit me further down the line. The extraordinary thing about coping with the death of someone close to you is that there is always so much to do afterwards: the funeral to organize, things to sort out. Being kept busy is very helpful.

I went back to *Strictly* the week after my father died. I think mainly out of loyalty to Brendan. I didn't want to let him down – he'd been so supportive of me over the last couple of months that I thought I should go back. On the first day of rehearsals, I was told I was supposed to dance a cha-cha to 'I Heard It Through the Grapevine' and then do a waltz to Frank Sinatra's 'Unforgettable'. I was really focused during the session and concentrated extremely hard on getting the steps down, but when I came home that night, it felt so inappropriate and weird. What was I doing? Why on earth was I carrying on? I'd only really been dancing for him, my dad, and now he was dead, there didn't seem any point to it all. I didn't have the stomach to try and win the show, and what for anyway? I couldn't care less. It was never about winning the show for me; that was all a big lie. I cared a bit about the points, but only so long as they meant I could stay on to dance a bit more for my dad, and now he was gone, my whole reason for being there was too.

It was all too much. I didn't want to worry about sparkly dresses. It was time for real life. The Frank Sinatra might have been beautiful to waltz to, but no one wants to cha-cha to 'I Heard It Through the Grapevine' a week after their father has died. No one at all.

I was just terribly confused. Should I make myself carry on with the show? Should I stop? But that would mean letting down Brendan. I wasn't really grieving at that point; the dancing was keeping me going as a matter of fact. I was upset, but the full reality of the situation hadn't really hit me. I felt like I could carry on, but I spoke to Billy, who said, 'Whatever you do, do *not* carry on.' I am not sure whether he thought he was giving sound advice or whether it was his green-eyed monster talking, but I decided he must be right and pulled out. The producers were disappointed.

And then I fell into a proper depression. I wasn't dancing any more and it all hit me. Not only had I lost my dad, I had lost my close friend Brendan; I was no longer working; I had nothing to do; it was freezing cold; it was December. It was just awful. Now what was I supposed to do? Sit around and cry? But I wasn't crying. I couldn't cry.

Throughout this period my relationship with Billy was quite tense. Billy suddenly started suggesting that I may be having an affair which in turn made me think that he might be having one and covering up by having a go at me. Anyway it was the last straw. Like I had had the time to be cheating on him while my dad was dying.

'Are you kidding me?' I said disbelievingly. 'I've just lost my dad. You are supposed to be the person closest to me. Really? Now? My dad died less than two weeks ago! It is not about you.'

I broke down. I cried and cried.

Billy picked a fight, but he picked the wrong day. This wasn't about him or his ego. This was about my mum, my brother and me, who'd just lost someone we loved. I was furious. He felt very distant from me then.

We had Christmas together, which was dismal. I didn't really want him there, and he certainly didn't want to be in my farmhouse in Kent. Then I had a bizarre electrical fire at the house, which Billy tried to put out with a hose! The damage was substantial. We lost power to the house. It was freezing and Billy suggested we fly to St Barts. It was his solution to any problem: if it felt too tricky, just get on a plane somewhere. So we spent New Year on the beach in St Barts, just the two of us, which felt terribly wrong. We hated each other and it was miserable. We had a few rows; it was the same old same old. Strangely, he didn't ask me to marry him at this point. I think he'd had enough. I think I was the *last* person he wanted to marry! He was not going to live in my farmhouse in Kent. I think I might have made his life too real: he'd done hospital, chemo, death, and now my house had burned down. Billy does St Barts; he does not do Rochester.

We flew on to LA, where he told me he had a job in

South Africa on a movie and I said, 'Go! Good. I'm glad you've got a job.'

I flew back to London. I didn't want to be in LA on my own. I started doing up my house in Kent, repairing it after the fire, and I moved back in with my mum. I didn't want her to be on her own, but equally it was really difficult. I hadn't lived at home since I was nineteen, and she was grieving which made her angry at times. Billy was also being difficult. He wasn't calling me, and when he did, he was evasive. Whenever I suggested I go to see him in South Africa, he avoided the issue.

So eventually I asked him straight: 'Are you having an affair?'

He denied it at first and then finally admitted it. He'd found some sexy young actress – younger than me and ready to be impressed – and I thought, Billy Zane, you are a fuckwit. The whole thing had gone full circle. The irony was, of course, I was three years older now and was perhaps ready to get married and have babies. I could now concentrate on our relationship. My dad was dead and I had the time. Only now he didn't want it. He was too busy getting tantric with another young woman, doing downward dog and reading Osho.

We split up at that point, but then Billy invited me on a trip to Sparta to witness him finally receiving his Greek passport! I went because I wanted to see if we could work things out, but as I arrived another woman was just leaving and I realized it really was over between us.

I was devastated and I was living back home, this time in the box room – my bedroom having been turned into a bathroom – but I was back where I'd started, living with my mum, grieving my dad, in the place I'd fought so hard to escape. It was horrendous. After all that I had been through, how had I ended up back here?

While I was living in my mum's house licking my wounds, at least I could focus on work. I'd changed agent in the UK and hooked up with the extremely talented Sarah Spear at Curtis Brown, who looks after the broodingly handsome Robert Pattinson, among others. She was incredibly supportive, and whereas before I had been dismissed as an underwear model who'd been on the telly, suddenly I started to be seen and auditioned and was offered some more interesting work, including *Hotel Babylon* for the BBC and *Moving Wallpaper* for ITV.

One of the most exciting jobs was Neil LaBute's *Fat Pig* at the Comedy Theatre in September 2008. It was my first West End production and I really enjoyed it. The first time I walked out on stage, the audience started clapping. It was such a warm response from people who wanted me to do well that I started to giggle.

Starring Nicholas Burns, Kevin Bishop and Katie Kerr, it was a proper serious piece of work on the West End – an experience I can now tick off my bucket list. I only wish I had invited my old headmaster Mr Vote from Italia Conti to see me. Not to rub it in in any way, because I actually know he would have been thrilled for me. It was what he'd wanted for me all along.

The first two weeks of the run were amazing, as indeed were the rehearsals, but it does get extremely repetitive after a while. Two weeks in, or three if you are lucky, it ceases to become an adrenalin-fuelled seat-of-the-pants terror ride and transmogrifies into a day job. Every night you try and find something different, but it can be boring. I remember corpsing on stage a few times, but it was all down to that Kevin Bishop. He was very naughty and used to rip off members of the audience every night. He would try and get in my eyeline when I was on stage and pull faces and mess around.

I got on extremely well with him. We had a proper laugh together. One evening, during the last week of the run, we had a massive night out and I drank way too much vodka. I was throwing up in my Hermès bag in the back of a taxi and I said to Kevin, 'You have got to get me into my home. I am not sure I can make it on my own.' So he pushed me in through the main door and guided me up the stairs. I was staying in a flat in Notting Hill which belonged to Julie Christie. It was a beautiful place with high ceilings and a little fireplace. It was all white and open plan with a four-poster bed and French windows that opened onto a square. It was a jewel-box. So as I was walking up the stairs that evening, I started taking off my clothes. To which Kevin looked horrified and yelled, 'I am married! I am married!' What he didn't realize, as he pushed me through my front door, was that I was taking off my clothes as they were classily covered in vomit.

I let myself into the flat, got into the shower and promptly curled up, fast asleep, stark naked with the water dribbling down my face. At which point the police came knocking on the front door to the building, hoping to arrest someone for being drunk and disorderly. Apparently the taxi driver had called them. Kevin would not let them into the building, so they took him off in the squad car to get the money to pay for the taxi to be cleaned, which he did, and then he went home to his rightly increasingly pissed-off wife, Casta. I remained oblivious to the whole thing, still snoozing starkers in the shower.

The next day, I woke up at midday, still drunk, terrified about the 2 p.m. matinee. All I could think was, Get to the theatre. Get to the theatre. When I arrived, everyone looked at me, and Kevin said, 'Oh, no one thought you'd make it.' I managed the whole show, and come the final scene, when I had to change, I was just so thrilled to finally get into the sodding bikini. When I walked out, though, everyone started to laugh and I couldn't think why. I looked down, and instead of wearing sandals with my outfit, I was still wearing my office shoes! I managed the whole thing, remembered my lines and hit my marks. I just had a minor wardrobe malfunction right at the very end.

But I survived the whole experience and added another string to my bow. The thing about a West End run is that you have to have stamina, commitment and character. You've learned the lines, turned up on time, found new things in the work every night, got on with people and, most important of all, got through it after a heavy night on the Absolut. It was quite a challenge. I'd love to do it a bit more. It was a world I liked. You come alive at 4 p.m., which is my time. I am not an early bird.

It was while I was in *Fat Pig* that I started dating Danny Cipriani. Our first encounter was in a rainy car park near Watford. He was leaving the Grove Hotel along with his friend Dizzee Rascal just as I was arriving for a drink at a computer games event with my manager, Jon Fowler, and some friends. We were introduced, we chatted for ten minutes, and that, in retrospect, should have been that.

They say that appearances can be deceptive, and

in my experience nothing comes in a more deceptive package than Danny Cipriani. When we met, he was a handsome, crooked-toothed, teetotal twenty-year-old who lived with his mum. Butter wouldn't melt in his mouth. Or at least so I thought. In those snatched ten rainy minutes we'd talked about music, ballet and the Royal Opera House. I didn't have a clue who he was, but I was absolutely smitten. It was only when he drove away that my agent told me Danny was a talented rugby player. In an uncharacteristically forward move, I asked my agent to pass on my telephone number. So in reality what happened next was my fault. I probably brought the heartache and heartbreak down on myself.

The next day, Danny called me and I invited him to the taping of an interview I was doing with Jonathan Ross. I was going on his show to talk about the launch of my new perfume, Vivacious; it was all very WAG! Danny turned up on time, dressed in a smart suit, and it was the first time that he lied to me. It was a little white lie, but a lie all the same. He told me he was twenty-one, when in fact he was the tender age of twenty. A full eight years my junior.

The relationship started off quite slowly. I was living in Notting Hill. Meanwhile, Danny was living at his mum's in Wimbledon. It was very casual. We were just dating. It was September 2008 and he was in training, hoping to be picked for the England team at the Autumn

Internationals, and I was at the theatre every evening. We were both very busy. He was up at 7 a.m. and out of the house pretty sharpish. He was playing for the London Wasps, so at weekends he would travel all over the country. He'd be in Newcastle one week, Manchester the next, Ireland the week after, and it was every weekend. But he still made time for me and would drive up from Wimbledon just to kiss me for five minutes at the stage door. It was very sweet and, honestly, quite blissful. He seemed perfect for me at the time: I wanted something light-hearted and fun, after two long-term relationships. Danny wasn't older, like Billy; he wasn't going to want to marry me; he wasn't going to want to have babies. He was interested in my career, but he had his own highly successful thing going on and was focused on his own work. When we weren't working, we could hang out and it was a perfect dynamic.

At that time Danny was the golden boy; he was going to replace Jonny Wilkinson. He was the next England superstar, but his rugby and his form changed when he met me. It was not down to me. He'd had a terribly injury earlier that year, when he'd broken his ankle, and was a lot more tentative in his tackling afterwards, as he had realized he was no longer invincible and wasn't made of tensile steel. But everyone thought it was because he was 'with Kelly' and must be having late nights out, showbiz-ing around, dining at the Ivy.

The reality was that I was in a play doing eight shows a week and not going out at all. There were headlines saying, 'Kelly Brook Will Make Sure Danny Cipriani Will Never Be the Next Jonny Wilkinson.'

Truth be told, I didn't know much about the world of rugby and was as surprised to be mentioned in the back pages of the tabloids as Danny was to be in the front. So I had to brush up on all that.

In November 2008, Danny replaced an injured Jonny Wilkinson in the number-10 shirt playing the Autumn Internationals, only to be dropped after three matches out of four due to poor form. That really affected him. It was all he had worked for his whole life. He'd had one bad game and couldn't understand why they'd dumped him. He'd given himself five out of ten, so it wasn't as if he didn't know he had work to do. But his attitude and immaturity were starting to become a problem.

He had already been dumped by the England team back in March, for inappropriate behaviour, when he'd been photographed leaving a club the night before an England game at 12.30 a.m., and this was all part and parcel of the same perceived attitude problem. In his defence, he behaved much better than most of the rugby players I met subsequently. I think they picked on him. I used to go to nightclubs with other members of the England team and there'd be players with their shirts off, surrounded by girls, going wild, but when

I first met Danny, he'd sit drinking pineapple juice and chatting to his mates. He wasn't a midget-thrower at all!

I understand rugby is a team sport and you can't have a bad egg in the team, but I think Danny found it very hard to fit in with the rest of them. He really struggled with that. For a start, he didn't drink alcohol, and he also suffered from depression. In the media, they said he wasn't taking his career seriously, which could not have been further from the truth. He never had a day off from training. If he wasn't at the club, he was on the track.

We had so many people who didn't want it to work. I think the relationship was doomed from the beginning. He was very young and it was casual – we were both busy people spending our limited free time just getting to know each other. I had no idea why so many people wanted to get involved and chuck in their penny's worth.

I heard that people around Danny were recommending that he stay away from me, as I was a 'user' and *such* a bad influence. Apparently, I was a gold-digger who used men and I was using our relationship to further my own career and get coverage in the press.

You had to feel sorry for Danny. He had no idea what to think. He had the people advising him criticizing me and he didn't know how to stick up for me, but at the same time he knew me and he knew I didn't use my relationships to get publicity. And we were both confused about how dating a rugby player would create the kind of coverage that was useful to someone currently doing eight shows a week on the West End stage! It was odd and frankly ridiculous! Everyone seemed to have forgotten that I'd been successful for over a decade by now – I didn't need Danny to help my career.

I remember when I first started out glamour modelling and people would ask me what I wanted to do with my life and I'd say, 'My dream is to be one of those finger-pointing models on *The Price Is Right*.' They wore glamorous dresses and were on the TV. Then all of a sudden everything I had wished for I achieved: I had wanted to be on a billboard; I had wanted to design my own clothes range; I had been desperate to make a film and star on the West End. It was almost like I couldn't dream big enough! But equally I would say to my mum, even as a little girl, 'When I am a Hollywood movie star, you can come and visit me and lie by my pool.' A lot of the time it was a bit of a joke, but the more I said it, the more it came true.

Do I think of myself as a feminist? If that means ambition is good, that women are as deserving as men and equal to them, then the answer is yes. Women can run their own businesses, and they can change their lives. Where you are born is not necessarily where you have to end up. Women can have it all. It is just nowhere near as easy as it looks. You don't have to be the product of your own environment.

However, when it comes to dreams and wishes, there is an expression that springs to mind: be careful what you wish for. And honestly, what you shouldn't ever wish for is a telephone call from Simon Cowell.

★

It was January 2009 and I was happy. I was smiling for the first time since my dad died, and I was in Harvey Nichols, minding my own business, wandering around vaguely looking at skirts and wondering if I should treat myself to some overpriced designer clobber, when I got a call from my agent.

'Kelly, we've had a call. Are you interested in being a judge on *Britain's Got Talent*? Simon Cowell wants to speak to you. I've given him your telephone number and he is going to call you shortly. There is someone else in the running, but apparently Simon is very keen on you.'

They hung up and I was still standing in Harvey Nichols, a pair of shoes in my hand.

I'd never met Simon Cowell. I'd watched *Britain's Got Talent* once, maybe twice in my life. I was aware of what *The X Factor* had done for Cheryl Cole and how it had reinvented her, after she'd been found guilty of assault, having smashed up a toilet attendant. I knew he could really change things, turn things around. But to be honest, I was quite happy – I didn't have anything I wanted to change; I didn't need anything turning around. I had just been nominated for a WhatsOnStage Award for my role in *Fat Pig*. I didn't have any pending court cases or skeletons dangling out of closets. Everything was great. I was not sure I wanted anything he could give me, so I carried on shopping, trying on some Louboutins. About twenty minutes later, my phone rang again.

'Kelly. Hi. It's Simon . . . Simon Cowell.' I think he paused just so I could take in the magnitude of his name, then he asked me if I'd like to be a star and said he could do the same for me that he'd done for Cheryl – he could change people's perceptions of me. I was quite taken aback. Perceptions of me? What did he mean?

I thought, You cheeky bastard! This was certainly the most cheesy conversation I'd ever had in my life. I think he wanted me to scream with delight down the phone because he had picked me! Simon had picked me! Thank you, Simon, for saving me from the hell of my own existence!

But all I could think was, The person he thinks I am and the person I actually am are so far apart that this is going to be tricky. I was going to turn thirty later that year; I'd lived a life. I wasn't twenty-two; I wasn't damaged or fragile or needy. I was a confident young woman with her own money who didn't need some rich powerful figure to sweep in and make it all better for her. I thought, I am not really sure how I am supposed to play this game. I am not sure what to do.

Against my better judgement, I agreed to join the show. I am not sure what I was hoping for, but it was definitely not what actually happened.

I was told I had to start the following day, so I put down my shopping, sat in a changing room on the second floor and hit the phone. I needed to get my team together, and quickly. I called my driver, Alan, and asked if he could take me up to Manchester, I telephoned my stylist, Marcella, and asked if she could call in as many clothes as she could that afternoon, and I asked my make-up artist, Ginny, if she could come to film in Manchester for four days or so. Before I'd left Harvey Nichols, I'd got my team together. I went back to the flat, said goodbye to Danny, and that night, I left.

I'd been promised a six-figure contract. Surely this was money for old rope? How tricky could it really be? On the way up, I spent the journey watching back-to-back YouTube clips of the show. It was hard to know who I was going to play – was I going to be nice Kelly or nasty Kelly? It was a lot to take in and I decided I was just going to be myself and see what happened.

We arrived and checked into the hotel. We were met by various people in production, but none of the other judges, or indeed the leviathan himself, Simon Cowell. The next day, I went into hair and make-up. I wore a nice 1950s dress that Marcella had found for me, just a hint of cleavage going on, nothing too over the top. I was the first to arrive. Piers Morgan was next.

The last time I'd seen him, many years earlier at a charity dinner, he'd been working for the *Mirror* and I had gone over to introduce myself. Only to have him be incredibly rude in return.

'Last time I saw you, you were making rather a lot of tabloid news,' he'd said.

'Sadly not in your paper,' I'd replied, as I had only really worked for the *Sun* and the *Star*.

'Yes,' he'd retorted. 'In the *Mirror* we only ever feature women with talent.'

So when he walked into the make-up room, my heart sank, as I thought, Oh God, here's that prick from the *Mirror*.

I did manage to smile and say hello, while he pretended we'd never met. I corrected him, reminding him that he'd told me I was a woman devoid of talent. He then roared with laughter and for the next ten minutes told everyone who came into the room the same story over and over again. How they all laughed! And how he loved telling the story. I think he likes to insult you, and his shtick is that you are then supposed to fall in love with him despite him being so rude to you. Which inevitably I did.

Next in was Amanda Holden. She was totally shocked to see me. She said no one had called her and told her that I was joining the gang. In fact, it turned out that none of them had been told there was to be a fourth judge. Naturally, all our reactions as we met for the first time were being filmed, so that they could be used for content. It felt like the judges were all being played, and you couldn't blame them if they found it rather annoying.

I had worked with Ant's wife before, as she was a make-up artist on *Strictly*, and I knew Dec a bit because we all knew Robbie Williams from a long time ago in LA. So when they arrived in make-up, I got out of my chair and made a big show of saying hello. I kissed them both and then asked, 'So what are you guys going to be doing?'

They looked shocked. They were *so* insulted by the question. Then Ant or Dec said, 'What do you mean? What do we do on the show?'

I hadn't meant that, of course, because I knew they presented the show, but I was being chatty and I wanted to know what they were doing and how it was going to work. But that was not how it had come out.

Simon arrived about four hours later with the most

beautiful make-up artist in tow. He was always followed around by the most stunning women. He came and sat next to me with a cigarette in one hand and an air puri-fier in the other. He also had a *huge* bag of what looked like vitamin pills and supplements. It screamed neurosis on every level.

It was all a little awkward, so I said, 'Nice to meet you.' I didn't really know why I was there. Did he fancy me? Think I had talent? Was a great TV presenter? I wasn't sure, but I just went with the flow.

I went down on the stage. Everything was OK. I was introduced as the fourth judge to everyone, and I was put next to Simon. What I didn't realize was that being placed next to Simon is a big deal. The first day was fine. I got on with it. I was a bit upset by some of the contestants who came through, as they clearly weren't very well, but Simon explained that sometimes these things happen and 'They slip through the net.' Then he turned to me halfway through filming and said, 'You're a singer, aren't you, Kelly?'

I looked at him and had an awful thought. Had he actually heard my demo tapes all those years ago, the ones Sasha had touted around, the ones that I had sung a little half-heartedly on, the ones that had got me pre-cisely nowhere? I panicked. Had he got some bloody plan to turn me into the next Cheryl Cole? I had no interest in being a pop star, and I had no interest in singing, and I was not going to be his bloody puppet, dancing and prancing around at twenty-nine years old. This was not happening. So I shut it down immediately.

'No,' I replied. 'I don't sing.'

'Are you sure?' he asked.

'Absolutely.'

At lunchtime, we all sat down in the green room and he started to quiz me about my love life. Did I have a boyfriend? Yes, was the answer. Did he have a girlfriend? No. Then we had a chat about his ex-girlfriend Terri Seymour, who was at Models 1 with my sister. We then discussed his schedule and how full on it was. He asked if I had seen the show. I said I had, but I didn't sit down every week to watch his TV shows, which was probably a little rude. But I didn't, so I was being honest.

The whole thing felt very odd. I don't know what was going on in Simon's mind, but the questioning had felt like a getting to know you audition – one that I'd failed! If that was the case, it would have been cheaper for Simon to just take me to dinner at the Ivy and be done with it! On day two, I was shunted down the row.

At the end of day two, I was standing in the lift with Piers when he said, 'So how do you think it is going?'

'Honestly, Piers,' I said, 'I don't think they want me back. I don't think it is going great.'

I had such an awful vibe off the producers. I don't

think they wanted me there; my fellow judges didn't want me there; Ant and Dec didn't want me there. In fact, I don't think anyone had wanted me there apart from Simon, and now I couldn't help feeling I had managed to turn him right off the idea.

I left at the end of the third day. I went back to London and then my agent got the call and rang me up and said, 'Kelly, I don't know how to say this, but they don't want you back.'

I was angry and hurt, and the first thing I said is not printable! 'So now what?' I continued. 'I have to deal with all the shit press? I hope they are paying the contract?'

'They are paying the full thing.'

'So it is just the press fallout we have to deal with?'

'Just the press.'

'Here we go again! "The Day *Britain's Got Talent* Was Titmatized By TV Bimbo Kelly Brook."'

The next day, it all kicked off. The producers announced, 'Kelly is fired after three days.' Everyone got very excited. It was a good way to launch the show. Total chaos. But they were all happy: I'd gone, they had their story, and everything was back to normal. The reason given for sacking me was that having four judges made the format too complicated (though today they've managed to uncomplicate things and have four judges again). Simon called me a couple of days later and intimated that he'd been under pressure to push me out and that some people had been jealous of me. I guess I'll never really know the full story.

I didn't care that I wasn't on the show. It was just the fallout that was so annoying. The press were camped outside my house again, and they just don't stop pounding the door, pounding you; it becomes exhausting. So I came out of my house, put on a nice pink dress and smiled for everyone. Then I said to Danny, 'I think I might just have to disappear off to LA. I won't be getting another TV job here anytime soon.'

So I flew to LA, and three days later, I was sitting having lunch at Shutters in Malibu, in a pretty yellow dress, eating fish and chips with Sadie, having just been house-hunting, when a film producer, Alix Taylor, who was sitting at the next table, came over. She asked me if I wanted to audition for a film, *Piranha 3D*. A month and a half later, I was in Arizona making a movie for Harvey Weinstein. It was the biggest movie of my career so far. It grossed over $100 million and I achieved a lifetime's ambition to be photographed on the front cover of *Playboy* by the fantastic Ellen von Unwerth. So I suppose, in the end, I have something to thank Simon for.

Making happy memories. When Dad had cancer I took him and Mum to Paris, including a trip to Versailles. Billy came too.

BELOW: With Dad in LA. I flew my parents over to stay before Dad had to start gruelling radiation treatment.

Strictly Come Dancing came along at the right time,
meaning I could stay in the UK and see Dad.
My dance partner Brendan Cole became a good friend.

In my dressing room on the opening night of *Fat Pig* at the Comedy Theatre, with my hairdresser Jonathan Malone.

My extremely brief stint on *Britain's Got Talent*. With (from left to right) Simon Cowell, Amanda Holden, Piers Morgan, Ant and Dec.

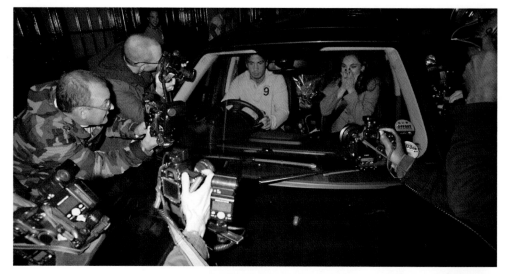

Photographers were
snapping my every move
with Danny Cipriani. I'd
never experienced that
level of attention.

With Danny in the Cotswolds.

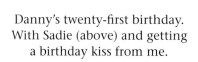

Danny's twenty-first birthday.
With Sadie (above) and getting
a birthday kiss from me.

With Riley Steele (centre) and Jessica Szohr on the set of *Piranha 3D*.

Filming the stunts for *Piranha 3D*.

With Danny and my cute little Rocky at the farmhouse in Kent.

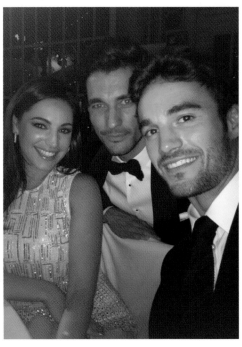

Thom Evans struck me as one of the nicest men I'd ever met.

With Thom and David Gandy at the *GQ* Awards.

With Thom in Santa Barbara.

Promoting *Keith Lemon: The Film* in Cannes. Leigh Francis is the perfect antidote to anything and everything.

In the dressing room at *Forever Crazy*, the French cabaret. I was a bona fide Crazy girl!

With my co-stars in *One Big Happy*, Nick Zano and Elisha Cuthbert.

Showcasing part of my 2014 swimwear collection for New Look.
Our collaboration has always been creatively interesting and productive.
And successful!

8

WAG World

It's thanks to Danny that I was dropped headfirst into a whole new world, one that was frankly ridiculous. WAG World. The life of a WAG is pretty thankless. Granted, there are the perks – the Louboutins (he bought me many), the designer handbags, the Hervé Léger frocks – but you are essentially living on your own, looking after a wayward child/boyfriend whose washing you occasionally see. They get up, go to training, get fed and come home at 3 p.m. five days a week, and then they travel every weekend to a different city to play. Welcome to the world of the rugby widow. They are either training or travelling, playing PlayStation or gambling. The only time you ever get to see them is in the evening. Either that or they are injured, in which case it is like having a caged animal in the house, sweating testosterone and acute anxiety about whether they will ever get back into the sodding team. Frankly, they seem to spend

90 per cent of the time frustrated, injured and not being picked for the team.

And there was a darker side to WAG World which I was completely unaware of at the start of my relationship with Danny. I had no idea about the appeal of the Premiership player. I had no idea that bagging these boys was considered by some women a basic career move to be executed immediately after leaving school. I had never heard of 'Mayfair girls'.

'Mayfair girls' are women who come down to London on the train from Birmingham, Leeds, Newcastle and Manchester, and go to the clubs and bars in search of footballers. That's all they do. They're professional. If they see another girl hitting on a footballer, they'll spike her drink to take her out of the game. They are ruthless. If they get a footballer's number, they'll bombard him with photos of their tits and their vaginas with their legs wide open. If they don't have anyone's number, they will bombard the guys on social media such as Snapchat, Instagram, Twitter and Facebook. They'll say subtle things like 'Come and fuck me.' Now, if you're a horny twenty-two-year-old footballer, or a rugby player in Dublin for the weekend, and there's a girl who's sending photos like that and who's willing to come to the hotel, what chance have you got as the girlfriend? You don't have a hope in hell.

What's more, with things like WhatsApp and Black-

Berry Messenger, or BBM, you can be constantly messaging people. They call it 'fishing'. So you can send the same message out to about ten girls and wait to see who is quickest to respond. It must be a godsend for some busy sportsmen.

It is no wonder that all these WAGs are *so* insecure, with their pumped-up lips, their pumped-up tits and weight issues. They are skinny as rakes because they are competing with an endless stream of vagina selfies. It's an impossible and hopeless situation.

Sportsmen are the new rock stars, and there are so many of them. So if you can't get a Chelsea footballer, or someone from Manchester United, you can probably get someone from Swindon FC and still have a nice lifestyle. There is so much money swilling around.

I'd been living in America; I'd only really dated actors, so this was a bit of a shock to me. I didn't understand the rules of the game at all.

I also had no idea the press would be so interested in the fact I was dating Danny. They got hold of what was going on very quickly and within a few weeks we had photographers outside my pretty Julie Christie flat snapping our every move. The media had decided to make us into the new Posh and Becks. He was an international sports hero, and I was the young London girl on the scene.

I have been papped ever since I was on *The Big*

Breakfast. I can't remember a time when they haven't been following me. When I move house or flat, it is normally only a matter of time before they arrive. In fact, more usually they are the first people to come round. Most of the time, I have one or two permanently outside the house. It's become worse because of the internet, rolling entertainment news and the rising demand for content. Now there are sites like the *Daily Mail* online, it is like living in *Big Brother*. They want to know what you are wearing on a daily basis, who you are with, where you are eating. They want to know absolutely everything. The likes of Kim Kardashian and Katie Price, with their reality-TV shows, have moved the goalposts so far that there is now no detail too small, no fact too banal, no observation too trite. The press think they are entitled to know everything because so many celebrities are willing to give them everything.

There are some celebs who do deals with the press and let them know where they will be and who they'll be with so they can make money. I don't do that. Everyone assumes I do, but I don't. Obviously I have my own agency that syndicates my photos from shoots, but I don't do deals with pap agencies, and I don't earn money from pap agencies. I am sure I could. I get called all the time by other girls asking if I know a pap's number so they can tip them off, but I don't.

Once in Barbados when I was on holiday with Danny,

we arrived at the beach and there was a whole load of photographers, so I asked them if they would leave us alone if I allowed them to take some photos of us on a jet ski. They agreed and that's what we did. I will do a deal like that. I will say to them, 'If I walk down the street and smile, will you leave me alone for the rest of the afternoon?' That is the most civilized way to deal with them.

Otherwise it is relentless. They follow you when you are walking down the street. You can't think straight; all you can see are six big blokes with cameras pointing at you. You're not looking at the street or the beautiful sky. You can't talk to the person you are with. All you can think is, how are we going to get rid of these paparazzi? It is completely suffocating and makes you very stressed.

These days, the paparazzi are much more in your face than they used to be. They follow you right up to your door and snap you struggling to put in your key. There is no law against it. There are no rules. You don't know the background of these guys. They can sometimes be scary, especially late at night when you come home after an evening out.

And once I started dating Danny, I got my first real taste of suffocating press intrusion. They wanted photos of Danny and me doing anything and everything together. They camped outside the flat, ran after us down the street and sat outside any restaurant we ever went into. Not that we went out much. But it put a huge amount of pressure on a couple of young people who were basically just trying to spend some time together and get to know each other.

I was more used to it than Danny, and I think it affected him more. It created a lot of jealousy and misunderstanding among his teammates. The rugby world suddenly saw him as more of a celebrity than a rugby player, and that was not acceptable in their culture. I got blamed, which I found a little weird. I had worked very hard in the world of media and entertainment, but they saw it as completely frivolous and not a legitimate business. They looked down on me and thought I was using him. His mother even suggested that my career suddenly took off when I met Danny.

Having been demoted to the Saxons (the England B-team) in May 2009, Danny went off to play in Colorado. He went from playing at Twickenham against the New Zealand All Blacks in front of tens of thousands of people to playing in Colorado, where the stadium was tiny and no one was watching. It was not even on the radar. It was such a high, followed by such a low. I think it happens often in sport, but it is a lot to cope with, especially when you are so young. And that's when he started to drink alcohol. For the first months of our relationship he was like an angel. He was healthy. He didn't drink. He was focused. He was great at rugby, beautiful to look at, great to be around. But then things changed.

I'd fled the UK after titmatizing Ant and/or Dec and the charming Simon Cowell, and was filming *Piranha 3D* on Lake Havasu in Arizona. It was an amazing few months working with my childhood heroine Elisabeth Shue, all these mad porn stars doing all sorts of things. I remember vividly one of the girls getting extremely drunk in a bar and hoicking up her skirt to show the director her vagina. No one, as I recall, batted an eyelid. We were there for Memorial Day in May, which is when what I called the Red-Neck Riviera comes out to party. It is a massive weekend when the young locals moor up their boats and get absolutely plastered. It is wild, everyone is tattooed, and they have pole-dancing poles on the boats. You have never seen anything like it. I too went wild. I am not sure if I went method or if the energy was infectious, but I was drinking. I got into fights; I was pulled out of bars; I was hanging out with porn stars; I lost it. I immersed myself in this world. All, of course, in the name of art.

Anyway, one of the actresses on the film, Jessica Szohr, who'd also been in *Gossip Girl*, was lovely and suggested we should go to Vegas for a little weekend break during filming. We arranged to meet her actor boyfriend, Ed Westwick, and Danny there. The Hard

Rock Hotel, where Ed and Jessica were going to stay, sent us a limo and we set off on the three-and-a-half-hour journey to Vegas. We ended up driving across the Hoover Dam, which was all dimly lit and, frankly, a little too *Close Encounters* for my liking. I remember asking the driver if he knew where he was going and he didn't sound terribly certain. It was eerie and weird and still miles from Vegas. A police car started trailing us and I suggested to the driver that we pull over to ask the policeman directions. He agreed and I got out of the car in my heels with my handbag. Then all of a sudden the police car slammed on the brakes and four coppers leaped out with their guns drawn, yelling, 'Get down! Get down on the floor!'

I froze and then started giggling with nerves. Perhaps not a great idea, as they yelled at me to get back in the car. We sat in the car with our hands in the air as they jammed guns through the open windows. I kept on giggling like an idiot, while Jessica hissed at me to be quiet.

'Shut up!' she said. 'They're going to kill us! They're going to kill us!'

Then one of the policemen went to the front of the car, opened the passenger door, yanked open the glove compartment and all these prostitute cards came tumbling out. All I am thinking is, Please God don't find drugs or firearms in here. We had no idea who the limo guy was or where he came from.

Eventually, we explained that we were actresses on our way to Vegas and the police cautioned us and told us that the next time we got pulled over, we were to *stay* in the car. In the US, you *stay* in the car. I presume they thought I was going to pull a weapon. Inside the car, you're contained and can't really do anything.

Anyway, this incident, coupled with weeks filming with porn stars, set the tone for our Vegas trip. We arrived and disappeared immediately into a club. We were so high after our meeting with the cops that we did shots and regaled anyone who'd listen to us with our amazing survival story.

It was *Gossip Girl* actor Chace Crawford's birthday. He'd just been crowned *People*'s 'Most Beautiful Person', so when he texted Jessica and invited us both to his after-party in his suite, of course we went! I stayed up all night playing drinking games and dancing around his three-bedroom suite.

I checked into the Wynn at about 7 a.m., and then Sadie and her boyfriend arrived from LA and we carried on to an all-day party at Tao Beach. It was 7 p.m. when I suddenly remembered, mid-tequila shot and sucking on a lime, that I had to pick up Danny from the airport, as he was flying in from playing rugby in Colorado. At this point, we'd quite a party going in our cabana and I thought it would be fun to take the whole lot with me to the airport. So we hired another limo and all jumped in. We found Danny at the airport standing there with his sports bag and a face like thunder. I got out of the car, obviously a little bit merry, a little bit Vegas, and I shouted, 'Ba-a-be!'

He didn't look pleased. The poor bloke got in the car and was introduced to everyone. Then someone suggested it would be a brilliant idea to go to Spearmint Rhino. Possibly me!

We were standing in the queue, my mate Sadie was there, drunk obviously, and Danny was trying to play catch-up, having knocked back whatever was in the limo at the time. Suddenly we spotted Frank Lampard and Beppe from *EastEnders*, so we shouted, 'Frank! Beppe!'

And we all joined up together. Sadie and her boyfriend, Matt, had a massive row and he disappeared off in a limo packed with porn stars, leaving her behind. Not that she cared much, as soon after she was sitting sandwiched between Frank and Beppe at a table with a glass of Cristal in one hand and a fist full of dollars in the other, having the time of her life.

I was with Danny and we both had a lap dance. Suddenly, the lap dancer stopped dancing on Danny and had a chat with him instead. Then she disappeared. Even through my exhausted stupor I thought it was a little odd, so I leaned over and said, 'Is everything OK?'

To which he replied he needed the bathroom. He

then disappeared off to the loo. My dance was finished, so I decided to go to the loo as well. On the way, I decided to try and find him, as he had been gone rather a long time. I'd not slept for two days and was quite drunk, and the club was very dark. I looked in various rooms and found nothing, so I gave up and went to the loo. While I was in the cubicle, on the other side of the door the missing lap dancer was chatting to her friend, saying how hot Danny was, how he'd given her his phone number. It was like a scene from a film. I came out of the loo and simply said, 'Hello.'

The girl screamed, 'That's her!' Then she changed tack and said, 'Girl, it looks to me like your boyfriend is a dawg. You need to get rid of him. That's karma right there, that is. Pure karma.'

'Yeah, girlfriend,' her mate agreed. 'You, like, *so* needed to hear that.'

As I headed back to the table, I saw Danny walking towards me.

'Babe,' he said, 'I've been looking for you!'

I punched him straight in the face! At which point, four bouncers leaped on me. They picked me up like the crazy, drunk, betrayed woman I was. It had all gone very *Jerry Springer*. I was then carried out of the club in my new cherry-print minidress. They held Danny back inside the club.

'This is domestic,' they said to me. 'You've got to go.'

I promised to calm down if they'd just let Danny go. I also asked them to get Sadie. They apparently approached her and asked if she knew a girl called Kelly, and like Judas, she replied, 'Nah.' She was sat with a glass of bubbles in her hand, having fun with Beppe and Frank Lampard; she was not moving for anyone. I was, rightly, not ruining her night!

Eventually, after about ten minutes, she came out and I told her what was going on and said we had to leave. I asked the bouncers once more to release Danny. Not out of the kindness of my own heart, you understand, but mainly because I wanted another pop at him!

'If you fight again, I will call the police. We don't do domestics here,' the bouncers warned me.

I swore blind, obviously. Crossed my heart and hoped to die. They released him. And as soon as I saw him, I launched myself at him. The bouncers held me back, and then Sadie bundled me into a taxi, with Danny jumping into another one and following behind in hot pursuit.

And then it got real.

Back at the hotel, I asked him what was going on. I was hearing whispers he was cheating on me and now there was this. But instead of talking to me, he disappeared into the bathroom. I heard a crash, and rushing in saw he'd knocked over a glass and had managed to cut himself. I asked him what the hell he was doing. He looked really upset.

'I hate myself,' he said. 'I hate myself.'

It really stunned me. I can see now that the focus had shifted and become about Danny's need for comfort, not about what he might or might not have done. That eventually became a pattern I think.

But at the time it seemed as if all the stress of the media had finally taken its toll. It might sound clichéd, but I actually wanted to help him. In hindsight, I now realize that he was making everyone around him feel the same. We were all running around after him trying to 'fix him' and make him feel better.

When I finished filming *Piranha 3D*, Danny and I both decided what happens in Vegas stays in Vegas and we'd try living together in London. We found a place to rent in Wimbledon, so we could be near his mother. I didn't want to upset her or exclude her. I am a family person and didn't want her to feel that she wasn't welcome anytime she wanted to come round.

Within two weeks of signing the lease I found out he was cheating on me. I was already committed to doing *Calendar Girls* at the Noël Coward Theatre, which my agent Sarah had put me up for in the autumn of 2009, and was now stuck in Wimbledon with a cheating Danny Cipriani, when I could have been in LA, in my lovely home, working. I was so depressed. A part of you dies when someone does that. I fell out of love with him at that moment, even though he promised it would never happen again. He went out and bought me a fawn pug, whom I called Rocky, as a sign of his contrition and commitment. It was really sweet but also exasperating. Rocky was gorgeous and I fell in love with him straight away, but I was away so much that I couldn't look after a dog, and our lease didn't allow us to have pets. In the end Rocky went to live with Danny's mum.

We spent the next few weeks like ships in the night, barely seeing each other. He got up early to go training, while I slept in. I'd get up at 11 a.m., and by the time he was home I'd be leaving for the theatre.

What kept me going was the fact that at the theatre I could put the problems with Danny to one side. I'd taken over from Jerry Hall and loved working with Helen Lederer, Arabella Weir and Julie Goodyear. They were all fabulous and great fun. We had a blast. I played Miss September, the one with 'considerably bigger buns', and I became quite friendly with the producer, David Pugh, who weirdly I bumped into at the Colombe d'Or a few years later. I was in Cannes promoting Keith Lemon's film when a gang of us decided to dress up and head out to Saint-Paul de Vence. I was dressed in some massive Liz Taylor earrings and a 1950s dress when I saw David having lunch with some other producers. He said, 'Hello, darling!' and then announced he had an idea for me to work at the National Theatre. Oh, how my Italia Conti bones shivered!

'I am putting together a team of the best clowns in the world,' he said. 'Rufus Norris to direct. You. Plus Toby Jones. I want to create the new Crazy Gang.'

The whole project has yet to come to fruition, but I did spend two weeks at the National being taught how to do Charlie Chaplin silly walks and Buster Keaton falls by the best mime artists in the world from Lecoq, which is a mime school in Paris. We even had a day with the Krankies, who were teaching us about playing to the audience and talking us through the early days of variety. They were extremely interesting to talk to and quite funny about travelling and working together, telling us how they insisted on separate dressing rooms, even though they're married, only coming together on stage.

At the end of 2009, however, my working relationship with Sarah came to an end. I wanted to focus on my business and commercial endeavours. The acting was fun and what I loved, but it wasn't regular or stable enough to keep me going. I like nice things; I spend money; I buy houses and sofas and new kitchens, bags and shoes. I needed to make money now, rather than hold out for the 'big acting job'. If I wanted to make money, the person to help me do that was Jonathan Shalit and his company ROAR Global, so that's where I went.

As part of my avoid Danny policy, I also signed up to

the *Strictly Come Dancing* live tour, which was going to start in mid-January. That would keep me out of his way once my stint in *Calendar Girls* was over! When that finished, I would be heading to LA for pilot season.

After a miserable Christmas, and while I was jiving my way round the country with my dance partner Matthew Cutler in February 2010, Danny announced he was going to Australia to play for the Melbourne Rebels when the new rugby season started. He knew he'd messed things up with me and the England team, and was hoping for a fresh start. We did have the conversation where I said if you want me to come with you, I will, and I am happy to come. We talked about both moving to Melbourne in the summer. I'd forgiven him by then and thought it could have been an amazing chapter in both our lives. Certainly it would have given him some perspective, having only ever lived in the UK. We even got Rocky his jabs and a passport.

But first I had to go to LA to promote *Piranha 3D* and Danny insisted he had time off and he wanted to come with me. I knew it was a bad idea, I knew he'd be a distraction, but he was really keen, so I said yes. I am not sure why I did. I no longer trusted him and felt he was always leading one woman or another along. This behaviour was both self-destructive and destructive to our relationship.

When I was in LA I remember taking him to a big

Hollywood barbecue and he went missing for half an hour – and in my head I just assumed he was off trying to find another woman to flirt with and lead on. In the end, it was all just too much, and I told him he could behave any way he wanted, it was his decision, but I couldn't be around him any more. I broke up with him – and two days later he was going out with Lindsay Lohan. He'd met her at the barbecue and hooked up with her as soon as I left town.

I knew Danny'd give his number out all the time. Sometimes he'd do it in front of me. I'd get invited to a *Vogue* or a Top Shop party and take him along, and he'd give his number out to anyone. I remember coming out of the bathroom and seeing him and Alexandra Burke exchanging telephone numbers. Now, I didn't want to overreact, but I had to ask, 'Why do you want her number, and why does she want yours?' He said she was going to fix him up with an iPad and then two months later – admittedly after we'd split up – they were pictured in the press going out on a date! But it did make me wonder if he'd just used me to make connections with all these famous women – women who, in a rugby world, you would never get to meet.

For the first eighteen months of our relationship I only caught him out once. But I was always suspicious of his trips to Monaco, his late-night phone calls to women who were 'just friends', his passcode always being locked on his phone. There were whispers from friends that he was a serial cheat. When I had first started going out with Danny, a woman had called everyone trying to get to me, to warn me that Danny was visiting her every week and had been for a while. She was very persistent. He had me believe it was a load of old rubbish, just a bitter ex-girlfriend. He swore to me that it had all happened before I met him and I believed him. If I heard any rumours I always questioned him and gave him ample opportunity to come clean but aside from that time before Christmas, he never did. All I could do was introduce him to a top sports publicist to keep his name out of the papers and have any press focused on his rugby.

In the end I always put his lateness and his unreliability down to the fact that he was laid-back. And of course I was famous, so if he did cheat, he'd be pictured somewhere, surely? And I loved him, so I didn't want any of it to be true.

Even though we'd split up, we stayed in touch. I still felt responsible for him and cared about his welfare. I was so busy worrying about him and hoping he didn't destroy his career that I forgot – I wasn't his mum!

9

Mr Nice and What Might
Have Been

My love affair with Thom Evans came at exactly the
right time. Or so I thought. It was 23 November 2010,
the night of my thirty-first birthday, and some friends,
including Jack Whitehall, and I had been celebrating
at China Tang, a restaurant in the basement of the
Dorchester. We'd finished dinner and the plan was to
meet Jenson Button in Mahiki, a club on Dover Street,
for a few more rum-based cocktails. Jenson was an old
friend and had just finished the Formula One season.
There was a whiff of pre-Christmas madness in the air
and everyone was in the festive spirit.

The club was packed, the music was loud, and the
Treasure Chest cocktails were going down a storm.
Thom was sitting at the next-door table with a group of
mutual friends and I remember thinking how very
handsome he was. Weirdly, I had read an article about
him the week before. About how he'd broken his neck

during a Six Nations game against Wales ten months previously, and how he had had to be stretchered off the pitch. His vertebrae were so badly knocked out of place he'd been a millimetre away from certain paralysis or even death. I remember reading his mother had taken care of him. A trained nurse, she'd stuck by her son and nurtured him back to fitness and he'd made a full recovery. I was very impressed by the story, his bravery and, of course, the dedication of his mother. I could not believe how strong and fit he was in the flesh. He seemed so healthy. He'd retired from rugby and was living in Weybridge and training to be a sprinter. He struck me as one of the nicest guys I'd ever met.

I don't think I spoke to anyone else that evening; not even the charming Jenson could tear me away. I left with Thom and from that night on we spent absolutely every day together. It was a very intense relationship and it drove Danny insane. Of all the professions to pick, of all the worlds to mix in, I had gone for another rugby player, albeit an ex-rugby player, and it annoyed him hugely. I thought they might vaguely know each other, but I had no idea they had actually played together for London Wasps. It was all a bit too close to home.

Initially, Thom took the whole Danny connection in his stride. I think because he'd had such a life-changing experience, breaking his neck, he was a little more sanguine and mature about things. His background was also very different from Danny's. In fact, they were chalk and cheese. Thom was born in Harare, Zimbabwe, and brought up in Portugal. His mum is South African, and his dad is from Manchester. He went to Wellington College, a smart private school, and played rugby, along with his brother, Max, for Scotland. Instead of feeling sorry for himself after his injury, he was engaged, upbeat and getting on with things. He was training with Margot Wells, a brilliant sprint coach in Guildford, thinking of getting into modelling and wanting to do an acting course in LA. I was about to go back to LA, as pilot season was kicking off again, so it was going to be a great opportunity to get to know each other.

Then I fell pregnant almost immediately. It was literally a few weeks after we'd met. We were being careful. It was just one of those things. It was a huge shock. I had been at the Dubai Film Festival and had started to throw up and feel faint, so I'd gone and bought a pregnancy test, half thinking I couldn't possibly be. I decided to wait until I was back home to take it.

And now it was Christmas Eve in Kent, and amazingly, it was snowing outside. My little house that I loved so much was looking amazing. I go mad for Christmas – perhaps because it was never that ostentatious when I was growing up – and I am a sucker for it all: I normally spend an absolute fortune. The girls from Nikki Tibbles's Wild at Heart, a florist in Notting Hill, come and do the tree, and I go all out with the food, the fire, the cards and all the trimmings. I even get the choristers over from the local church to sing carols. And this year I'd taken a pregnancy test and it had come out positive.

I remember calling Thom to come down from upstairs and saying I wanted to tell him something. I was rather terrified about how he would react. We had been going out with each other for exactly a month. Just over four weeks. It was all far too soon.

We sat down in front of the fireplace. I said I thought I was pregnant but wasn't sure and needed to see a doctor. Amazingly, Thom took it all in his stride. He said he was pleased. We were both totally shocked. I was hoping I'd made a mistake, as we hardly knew each other.

On Boxing Day, we flew to Portugal to meet his family, who lived in Abulfiera. They were absolutely charming and welcomed me very warmly into their home. The following day, we went to his local family doctor. We lied and told his parents we were going to watch the sunset, but in fact we had gone to get another test done at the doctor's. It too came back positive. I was definitely pregnant! It was a lot to digest, and as we walked back to the car, we decided we wouldn't tell anybody; we'd keep it to ourselves. I think partly it was a way of protecting ourselves, but also it was a way of giving us some time to absorb what was going on and think about our options.

Honestly, I think I was also still involved with Danny, not on a day-to-day level, but I was still emotionally invested in him. Thom and I would have been great just dating, hanging out in LA, going to the beach, doing auditions, power-walking through the streets, drinking buckets of latte. I didn't think he was anywhere near ready for a child. He was twenty-five, and things were just happening for him. He was just starting a new chapter in his life after his rugby accident. But he said he adored me and wanted 100 per cent to have a baby with me. I didn't want to have a termination, and so that was that. My US agents had interest lined up, it was pilot season again, and all of a sudden I was living in LA, with Thom, expecting a baby.

Being in LA, far away from home and the prying eyes of family, friends and, most importantly, the press, the pregnancy was easy to keep secret. No one really knew we were going out with each other, let alone having a baby.

Part of me enjoyed that, living in a bubble, pottering around, while Thom was studying at the Lee Strasberg acting school and always on hand, sweetly looking after me.

However, the rest of me was terrified. My hormones

and emotions were all over the place. Thom was adamant he wanted me and the baby; meanwhile, I was getting drunk and needy phone calls from Danny in the middle of the night from Australia which kept our emotional connection alive. I felt very trapped, and to top it all, the pregnancy wasn't easy. I was sick a lot. I had melasma, the mask of pregnancy thing. My whole face was red and blotchy and patchy. I had spots on my chest. Literally every side effect from pregnancy you could have I had! I was tired, throwing up, itchy and hideous. I wasn't in a baby-doll doing the dusting, gently taking a tray of tasty cupcakes out of the oven; I was mostly hunched over the toilet bowl hurling my guts up. I never glowed, and I never looked beautiful! And my mind was racing. I kept thinking, What would it have been like living with Danny in Australia? It was irrational, I know, but it might have been fun. It might have been interesting. Different. I might have been free. I'd had a fabulous life before Thom: I was single, and I could pick up and leave whenever I wanted to. I was so very scared, I think, of losing all that. I felt trapped and totally depressed. There were some days, and indeed a whole week, when I could not get out of bed. Even the smell of Thom made me feel sick. I used to have to change the sheets every time he stayed the night.

Fortunately for him, we were not living together, as he had a flat down the road, but he would come every day bringing groceries. I'd open the door, mumble, 'Hi,' take the bag, close the door and go back to bed. It was hell for both of us. In retrospect, I can't help but think I must have had prenatal depression. I didn't want to see anyone, go out or speak on the phone, and I was consumed by anxiety.

I was now doing the biggest, most important thing of my life with someone I didn't know, someone I'd met in a nightclub four weeks before Christmas. I was worried. Thom and I hadn't been through anything serious together. I didn't know how he was going to react if anything terrible ever happened. What if the shit really did hit the fan? That thought just scared the life out of me. I didn't feel trapped because I didn't want to be with him; I felt trapped because I was scared, scared of the unknown.

We were forced into announcing the pregnancy to the media slightly earlier than planned after I was snapped with a massive belly coming out of Fred Segal's on Melrose. I was squinting into the sun and wearing a peach V-neck jumper. Not a good look at the best of times, but especially not when you are four months pregnant. I looked *so* fat. I got a whole load of weird phone calls from the UK asking me if I was OK, suggesting very tentatively that I might have put on a few pounds, that I might have suddenly developed a serious binge-eating problem, or an acute Dunkin' Donuts addiction. Well, that was that. It was much better to tell them that I was pregnant. So when the next person called saying, 'You seem to have put on a bit of weight,' I barked back, 'Yes, well, I am four months pregnant – that's why!'

Thom and I were leaving for Bermuda on holiday the next day and the press were never going to find us there. I had started to feel a little better and a little happier about things. Perhaps my depression was lifting. I was re-joining the human race. In fact, I was a little euphoric. So it was actually a good time to announce my pregnancy. I took to Twitter just before taking off from LAX. I knew I was having a girl, and we could announce it all and spirit ourselves away. It was perfect.

After the holiday, Thom started to make noises about wanting to move back to the UK. He'd finished the Lee Strasberg course but felt quite disillusioned after being asked to go down on all fours and speak in a goat voice to a guy playing Jesus. He wanted to buy a house near Weybridge in Surrey where he had friends. While we were deciding what to do, we went to stay with his parents in Portugal. I'll never forget I was sitting on the sofa watching TV when the baby kicked for the first time. Everyone was so delighted they all gathered round to see if they could feel. I was thrilled. After all the depression and confusion, I was actually having a baby and it was exciting to feel it for the first time.

This was obviously not an ideal situation for Thom's parents – they barely knew me and yet I was having their granddaughter – but they were incredibly support-ive, generous and kind. I am sure it was not quite what they wanted for their son because he was so young, but we, and they, just got on with it and they were very nice. In fact, I could not have wished for a more sup-portive family. If you were to have a baby with anyone, you could not have picked a nicer man or a nicer group of people to surround yourself with. I was lucky.

It was just after the royal wedding, which was on 29 April 2011 – William and Kate had delighted the nation by tying the knot, and Pippa had stunned us all with her curves – when Thom suggested we go to Scot-land to see his brother, Max. I was six months pregnant and didn't really want to go. It was rather a lot to cope with – flying, staying in a hotel – and I really didn't fancy it. I was much happier nesting in Kent, and the garden was quite frankly rather nice at that time of year. I was enjoying pottering and watching the spring flowers grow. But Thom was keen, so we flew to Glas-gow, and even though his brother has the most stunning house, he put us up in a lovely hotel, which was very kind and thoughtful of him. It was Max's wife's birthday and we went to the house for a party in the evening. It was fun; there was lots of champagne and some nice people. Then they all decided they wanted to go out clubbing. I really couldn't go. I was trying to look after myself. I was tired after the flight. I wasn't drinking and I'd had enough, so I went back to the hotel to bed.

Thom came back about 2 a.m. or something, not terribly late. About 6 a.m., I woke up suddenly and there was blood all over the bed. I woke him up and told him something had happened. His face went white as he took in the blood all over the sheets. Something was seriously wrong. I went to the bathroom to try and clean myself up a bit and asked Thom to call an ambulance.

'Don't worry,' he said. 'I haven't drunk very much. It'll be quicker if I drive you.'

We got in the car and he drove to the local hospital, which was about five minutes down the road. When we arrived, they immediately turned us away, saying they didn't have the right equipment for me and that I should go to another hospital further away. It was 7 a.m. and I was quite reluctant to get in the car again and asked if they could call me an ambulance in the hope that I'd be seen more quickly. By this time the bleeding had stopped and they could see I was feeling a little better, so they suggested that we drive. They gave me no cause for alarm. Perhaps it was nothing after all. Even so, we went to another hospital, where I was admitted and put into a bed. Which is where I stayed for two hours. No one came to see me. I sat there for another hour and a half and was still not seen. There were no doctors, no nurses. There were no patients even; the ward was empty. No one took my pulse, my blood pressure, nothing. No one even suggested a scan. I was sitting on the bed, with Thom asking me what he should do. All I knew was that I didn't want to be there. If anything happened to me, I didn't want it to happen there.

Eventually, it was about 10 a.m. and I could call my own doctor in London. I asked him if he thought I'd had some sort of placental abruption and he said he needed to see me right away and asked if I could get back to London. All I wanted was my own doctor to see me. I checked myself out of hospital and got the first flight back to London with Thom.

I wasn't in any pain, there wasn't any more blood, and I could still feel the baby moving, but I was exhausted. I just wanted to lie down. I wanted to get home and relax. As soon as I got through my front door I went to bed. After about an hour, I woke suddenly. My heart was pounding. I sat up and immediately my waters broke. I was only six months pregnant; this was not supposed to be happening. I called an ambulance and said, 'I think you'd better come.'

I was very scared and felt something was seriously wrong as I shuffled into the ambulance, wrapped in a red blanket.

'You need to slow down a little bit, you do,' said the

229

paramedic as he closed the door. 'You can't live your life when you're pregnant.'

'You don't know anything about my life,' I replied, my heart pounding with rising indignation.

'I know exactly who you are. I've seen you in the papers, going in and out of restaurants and parties. You can't do that when you're pregnant.'

I couldn't be bothered to reply. All I could think was, How dare you? I am having a miscarriage right now and you're lecturing me on my lifestyle. You have no idea about my life. The truth was, I hadn't been out in months.

Eventually, I arrived at the hospital, where, unlike the paramedic, the staff were extremely kind and sympathetic. They examined me and confirmed that my waters had broken; they said to me that I would probably go into labour within the next twenty-four hours and I needed to consider my options. I couldn't believe it. It was like a nightmare. They said to me that if the baby came out breathing, they could wrap her in a blanket and give her to me, or they could take her straight to intensive care, but at around twenty-two to twenty-three weeks, the survival rate was low, and the survival rate without complications was very low indeed. It was a lot to take in. I remember saying I wanted it to be as natural as possible. What will be will be. I really didn't want any intervention or for the baby to suffer.

Because I was around the six-month stage, everyone was torn between whether this should be seen as a miscarriage or a stillbirth. In my mind, it was a miscarriage. That was how I was going to deal with it. But the hospital were insisting otherwise. I am sure they were following some sort of protocol, but it was not what I wanted at all. They kept on asking me for a name. Thom and I had yet to even discuss this. I must give them a name, they said. Thankfully, my mum was there to give me some moral support and we both said, 'No name.'

They kept on asking me if I wanted handprints and footprints, and I had to keep saying no. But they kept cautioning me, saying that I might come back in six months' time and have changed my mind. Why didn't I do it just in case? Still I kept on saying no. If I'd had my miscarriage two weeks later, I would have had to register the birth and death at the same time, which I thought was far too much to handle. So my mother and I were very much on the same page. That this was a miscarriage. Looking back, I was trying to detach myself – with love – for the sake of my own sanity.

I was sent home to wait for the miscarriage to happen. My mother stayed with me and made me soup. It was all very quiet and sad. None of us had anything very much to say. Then I felt some cramps in my stomach and I remember thinking, Here we go. We rushed back to the hospital and I had to give birth.

There were nurses all around, telling me how to breathe.

In the end, on 6 May 2011, sometime in the late afternoon, our baby girl was born dead. Any decision to make was taken out of my hands. They just took the baby away. I didn't take prints of her hands or feet or give her a name. Everyone felt very empty and upset.

Afterwards, the nurses were so kind. They warned me that my body would carry on thinking it had a baby to feed. They told me my milk would come in and that I'd need to put cabbage leaves on my boobs to stop them from feeling so hot. It was the most painful thing. I was bedridden for the next two days with these enormous boobs, covered in cabbage leaves. Apart from the physical fallout, I think emotionally the hormones affect you much more than you think they will. Much more than I have ever really let on.

Thom and I spent a lot of time crying that week. Ironically, something that had been such a shock and so unplanned had become something we'd both been desperately looking forward to. We'd been on a highly charged, very emotional journey together and for it to end the way it did felt cruel and truly devastating.

I often think that my relationship with Thom was slightly like a life lived backwards. He had never really known me other than as someone who was pregnant, irritable, unattractive and now obviously extremely sad and vulnerable. We hadn't had the chance just to be a normal young couple, have fun, go out, be a little bit careless and indeed carefree.

So we decided it was time to make a fresh start, put it all behind us. We rented a pretty flat that overlooked a communal garden in Maida Vale. My focus was on trying to get healthy, helping Thom with his career as a male model and actor, and getting back to what I did best.

Shooting *Keith Lemon: The Film* in Ireland was the perfect antidote to everything. In fact, Leigh Francis himself is the perfect antidote to anything and everything. Naughty, funny and loyal, he has become one of my very closest friends. I adore him. He makes me properly laugh, and that's exactly what I needed at the time. I remember seeing the script for *Keith Lemon: The Film* and I reacted in much the same way as I'd done to the outrageousness and hilariousness of *Piranha 3D*. Keith Lemon was so silly and naughty I wanted to do it immediately. Also, the part was not exactly taxing – I was playing myself, albeit an exaggerated panto version of myself, and I really enjoyed it. It was the beginning of a great friendship with Leigh and also led to me working with him on *Celebrity Juice*.

It was during the filming of *Keith Lemon* that Thom proposed. I'd been booked to fly to Belfast that morning, but suddenly my flight was cancelled, so I returned to our flat in Maida Vale and there he was. He'd bought a beautiful ring, a vintage 1920s diamond, and I immediately said yes.

Interestingly, or so it had turned out, when the shit did hit the fan, Thom had stood the course. The doubts I'd had about what sort of man he was when I first became pregnant had proved to be unfounded. He was loyal; he was kind and supportive; he hadn't left me in the hospital. In fact, the miscarriage had actually brought us closer together. It bonded us like I had never bonded with anyone before; it was trauma on a different level. He had seen me at my most vulnerable and my most disgusting, and had stayed. And so I decided he was 'the One'. I was thirty-two and really did want to have a baby. I was ready, and he really was a good person to have a baby with.

We both decided that we should keep our engagement a secret because we didn't want any media intrusion.

Excited and slightly nervous, I went to see my doctor, who said to me, 'Kelly, the best way to get over this is to try and get pregnant again. You aren't getting any younger and I think you should go for it.'

So Thom and I weren't careful, and just before Christmas 2011, I got pregnant again. I don't know if it was too soon, or if it was too much, but the look on Thom's face when I told him said it all. I think he was terrified. It seemed to me as if he was reluctant and given our previous experience I got that. It was like 'Here we go again', and indeed, we did go again. I had another miscarriage after a few weeks.

It felt like Thom was suddenly done with the whole baby thing. Having a miscarriage is hard on the emotions and I think it made him reassess what he needed. I think he wanted a job; he wanted a career; he wanted to know where he was going in life. I got the feeling he really didn't want this any more. And I have to admit that hurt. I know from experience that pregnancy is a rocky road and you have to be with someone who wants it too or the experience can drive you apart.

Our relationship limped on, both of us unhappy and fighting more. Thom had to drive a lot to Guildford to train. But we were still engaged in November 2012 when I starred in *Forever Crazy* with the Crazy Horse cabaret on the South Bank. I had been obsessed with the show ever since I'd seen it in Paris about two years previously, when I'd gone on a girls' weekend, staying at my favourite hotel in the world, Hôtel Costes, with my friend Tanya.

We'd decided to go to the Moulin Rouge and the Crazy Horse. Both were fantastic. The Moulin Rouge was huge, very commercial and incredibly professional. It was amazing to look at, but it was a little bit slick and somewhat cheesy, with nothing too risqué or challenging. The girls are fabulous, with legs up to their armpits, but it was a touch old-fashioned and slightly rammed to the rafters with clammy-handed businessmen for my taste. But the Crazy Horse was something else. Dita Von Teese was working an oversized martini glass in a manner that was so sophisticated and sexy it took my breath away. I loved it. The vibe was much cooler and hipper than the Moulin Rouge; it was half lit, with delicious cocktails and a much more intimate vibe. The show was incredible. A lot of the choreography has been around for decades, and the girls are very carefully chosen to look exactly the same. They all have to be the same height and weight, and their nipple-to-shoulder ratios have to be identical, so when they dance, you can't tell one from another.

Tanya and I went backstage after the show and I started chatting to the woman who ran it and asked her if she had ever taken the show to London, and she said not so far. So I announced, or rather put it out there in the universe, that 'One day I will do this show in London!'

And lo it came to pass. I heard a couple of years later that the legendary producer Harvey Goldsmith, from Live Aid, had got the London rights to the show and was planning to put it on at the South Bank. I don't think the tickets were selling hugely well, as no one in the UK really knew what the Crazy Horse was, so I rang up and asked if I could be in the show. Let's say they were not averse to the idea. They attached my name to it and we sold out immediately, extending the run for another two weeks.

I loved the whole experience. I got to hang out and meet all the dancers. I did the lip dance, using a juice-red pair of lips that were designed by Salvador Dalí, and I got to work with a choreographer who was an ex-Crazy Horse dancer and who had been with the company for over twenty years. I learned how to be a bona-fide Crazy girl. The dancing, the discipline and how you have to go to boot camp to learn all the routines – I loved it. Sadly, I don't have the measurements of those girls, so I was only really able to do a guest slot rather than the famous London guards number, when they dance semi-naked with their boobs out. I was desperate to do that. It's a throwback to those Italia Conti days. But I loved being backstage with the girls, getting ready and sharing make-up.

They all used to arrive looking like grungy French students, smoking fags out the back, and the transfor-mation was amazing. It was pure artifice, which is why I think I found it all so beguiling. They curled their hair, popped on the eyelashes and the regulation 'Russian red' lipstick they all have to wear. It was extraordinary to watch. They painted hair on their *faffoon* (a French word for 'pussy') with black paint to make sure they all had a neat triangle. They would sit there with their legs akimbo chatting away, slapping on the paint. They had amazing athletic bodies and were weighed every Sunday to make sure they stayed that way. In the Crazy Horse, you are not allowed to put on weight or to lose it. Everyone has to look the same.

The show wasn't burlesque, it was French cabaret, which is more routine-based, and was very slick and fabulous. I felt like I had run away and joined the circus, which was exactly what I needed at the time. I wasn't topless in the show – I didn't want to go topless, as it would have been another one of those deathly dull 'Kelly's boobs' stories, which I couldn't be bothered to deal with. I wanted to be part of the gang, and I *was* part of the gang. In the end, I was given an extremely prestigious red Crazy Horse bathrobe.

Thom came to see it. I am not sure what he thought; he never really said.

Not long after that, he and I split up. His modelling career was picking up, he'd been on the front cover of a few magazines, and a big agent in the US wanted to represent him. He was excited and so was I; after all, this was what we had both been working towards for a while. The last thing I wanted was for him to be hanging around the house, sitting on the sofa, while I went out to work. It was important that he found something to do after his rugby career and the sprinting hadn't gone anywhere.

I suggested we rent a flat in LA (I'd sold my LA house) so that I could go and visit. I was booked to appear on *Celebrity Juice* with the fabulous Leigh Francis, to cover for Fearne Cotton, who was on maternity leave, so I couldn't immediately go to the US with him. I was incredibly hurt when he said he wanted to go to LA alone. He didn't want to be weighed down by a flat. He wanted to bum around, 'work it' and see how far he could get. When I brought up the subject of marriage and children, the colour drained from his face. It was clear it was the last thing he wanted. He said he wanted to be an actor and focus on his 'new life' in LA – a wife and child would only slow him down. He didn't want to be in a relationship any more. It was obvious!

We had an almighty row. Thom was lovely and calm and gorgeous most of the time, but when he got angry he got really angry. That last night was not the first time he'd lost his temper, but it was the last straw. There are people who can handle – even enjoy – shouting and rows, but I heard enough in my childhood to last me a lifetime and when I see it as an adult, I run a mile and I run fast. The very first time I experienced one of Thom's outbursts, I mentally backed off, and it was like walking on eggshells for ever after. I think for pretty much a year after the miscarriage, that was how I felt.

But that night something inside me snapped and I fell out of love with him in an instant. I kicked him out of the flat and announced very calmly that I was going to stay in a hotel and was never coming back.

I was not a wholly innocent party by any means. I shouldn't have kept up my friendship with Danny. Thom felt threatened by him. Danny was still playing rugby, while Thom's career was over. I am sure he would have loved to have been in Australia playing rugby and shagging lots of girls; instead, he was with this thirty-two-year-old girlfriend who'd had two miscarriages and now wanted to settle down and have children. I was not the fantasy.

Thom went to LA and never asked for the ring back. I didn't cry and I didn't speak to him again. Within a month he'd hooked up with someone else, a well-known actress on American TV. He was reportedly 'smitten', appearing on the cover of *Hello!* two months later announcing she was 'the One'. I am sure he will do well. He did thank me for helping with his career and I wish him all the best.

In retrospect, all I can think is how exhausting, time-consuming and ultimately fruitless the whole episode was. It was a traumatic and physically draining two years. And for what? How could I have done all that *and* run my business at the same time? Imagine what I could have done if I hadn't been weighed down. What else could I have achieved if I hadn't been so distracted? Nothing short of world domination!

I remember my mother saying something to me as I was lying in hospital immediately after I'd had my first miscarriage.

'Everything is going to be fine, Kelly,' she said, patting the back of my hand. 'He's not going to be around for long.'

I think she knew on some level that our relationship wouldn't last. Not that he was a bad man, quite the opposite, but we weren't right for each other.

It wasn't until after a two-year break and when Danny returned from Australia in early 2013 that we decided to give our relationship another go. The passion had never gone and I felt there was unfinished business between us. He was a complicated, sexy man-child who I wanted to figure out, and I'd never quite felt I'd had him all to myself. And surely he'd grown up in the last eighteen months.

Danny was living in Manchester and playing for Sale Sharks (a north of England rugby team) so we weren't living together but we spent as much time together as we could. I wasn't sure this relationship was going to be a forever thing, but Danny always goes full steam ahead and was already saying he wanted to marry me. He loved me – I knew that – but he was alone so much of the time he craved attention from anyone who was willing to give it. And there were plenty.

It started again, the late-night phone calls, all the signs someone might be cheating on you which you explain away because you don't want to believe it. But increasingly I just couldn't ignore it. One Sunday afternoon during August 2013, Danny was about to start his second season for Sale Sharks. If I was going to continue with this relationship, I'd be up and down on a Virgin train to Manchester three to four times a week, playing the ever-loyal rugby WAG. A huge commitment in anyone's books. And to be honest, I didn't really want to do it. I didn't think he was worth it. But I needed the proof. I needed to be sure that my instincts were right, that he was a serial love rat and no effort on my part would ever be enough. So I got hold of his phone, bit the bullet and went through the lot.

Anyway, it was extremely sad to see how Danny operated. I think he just wanted attention, attention from every girl he liked the look of. Most of the time it was not sexual. It was just a game of 'Can we meet?' to see if they would be willing.

It was endless. I wasn't shocked; I was just confused. Surely they didn't all think they were the only one? So I decided to call them. One by one. I knew I wasn't going to get any answers from Danny – I am not sure I ever got a straight one.

The first was Jemma Henley, a tattooed model he had met through Katie Price. She had a surprisingly sweet voice. Her look was all porn, tattoos and just pure filth. She said to me they had kissed and she apologized. She later did a kiss 'n' tell revealing how they'd romped dozens of times behind my back, but on the phone she was as sweet as pie, probably thinking at some point he would be her boyfriend and not wanting to lose his trust. I informed her that she was, so far, one of six girls I was calling that afternoon.

The second woman was more wholesome-looking. At first, I couldn't make out if this was a sexual relationship, so I started to message her pretending to be him. I then sent a naked picture from Danny's collection (of Jemma) asking if it was her, knowing full well it wasn't. She called his phone immediately. I answered. She sounded very upset and was adamant that she had never met Danny and it was just a message relationship. She said she had no intention of meeting him, although sometimes his messages to her were of a sexual nature. She ended up also coming forward and selling her story that week.

You could not work out Danny's type from all these women. Probably just that they were responsive was all that mattered. There were young women and old women. Married women and single women. Even the mother of one of his friends. I kept going, calling up four more women, until I realized that I could potentially be hurting other innocent parties. Some of these women had children who didn't need to get dragged into this mess. It was definitely time to get out. For good.

I probably wouldn't have done any of this if Danny had just come clean about cheating. I was absolutely sick of being treated like a fool. To think all these women were running around with Danny having kicks and giggles at my expense made me sick. He did not really want to be in a relationship with anyone. At all. So it was just a kinky fix, a game, an addiction. 'A dirty secret', as he liked to call it.

It was all so beyond anything I'd ever expected to find that I just went out for a long walk around the block, feeling numb. All in all I spent three hours on his phone. I never even shed a tear. One of Danny's mates happened to call Danny's phone and so I asked him to explain what the deal was with athletes and their egos and why so many were unfaithful.

'Why is it,' I said, 'that with you guys you're either wanting the slut or the wife? Why can't you let a woman be everything?'

'No one has everything,' he replied.

When I got home, I confronted Danny, asking him how he found the time to do anything else.

'This is why you don't own a home,' I said. 'This is why you don't wash your clothes. This is why you are so lazy all the time that you can't even flush your own turd down the loo. You spend all your time on the phone pursuing women. I don't have time to do that. If a bloke sent me a picture on my phone, I wouldn't respond, and if I did, it would take hours. I am far too busy working or paying my bills to be bothered with that stuff.'

'I don't know what is wrong with me,' he said. He then looked at me and said, 'You don't even care. You're not even crying.' I wasn't. I had seen this all before.

By that point I just wanted every trace of Danny gone and out of my life. To me he was playing dangerous games and putting me, and all these women, at risk. I don't think every girl who goes out with a guy expects him to be 'the One' and declare his undying love, but if they do – and I suspect Danny did to every one of them – then it should be the truth. I am not saying girls don't enjoy sex, because they do, and sometimes a few dates and a bit of fun is fine. But when a guy talks a big game, it sends funny chemicals to our heads and we start imagining a future and laying off other potential suitors. It's a cruel, controlling game. It's not the way to behave, as people get hurt.

But that's Danny's game and how he gets women. He has no great banter or repartee; he's not a wit, bursting with intelligence, so the standard 'I love you. I miss you. I want your babies. Let's get married' is what he falls back on. It is enough to make any reasonably sane woman conjure up all sorts of fantasy scenarios. We do his job for him; we fill in the blanks and then wonder why we get hurt. Ultimately, it's bollocks.

Here I am, writing all this and taking the moral high ground as if I was the One. His One. The Chosen One. The love of his life who he lost due to a silly mistake, a misunderstanding, a moment of weakness, and all these bitches just got in the way of our living happily ever after and having it all. The reality is, I am one of them. One of many. He loved me no more or less than any of them. He spent just as much time making love to me as he did them, and communicated with them as much as he did with me. Yet I'm the public girlfriend. The one who made him look normal, together, a good guy. I took all the shit. Everyone blamed me for his failure, for his partying, when in reality he was just out chasing other girls. I let it go on for years and protected him from being caught out until enough was enough and I couldn't do it any more.

He'd had all of me, and I guess that was the problem: I bored him. Eventually, I realized in our final six months together that I had let him get away with too much. I had been a fool to myself. I'd played it too straight when I think what he craved in a relationship was the chase, the thrill, the new. Sex. And danger. But it had taken me years to work out what was really going on. What a waste of time.

Who knows what Danny really felt about any of us? That Sunday when I managed to get his passcode and spend a few hours in his world to see exactly where I fitted in, I realized I was no different from the others. We were all dealing with the same person and all fell in love with a messed up immature man who loved no one but himself.

I'm happy I got to the bottom of it all because for a long time my ego made me believe I was different. I wasn't. He was late not because he was laid-back; he was late because he didn't care. He had us all lined up ready, so when he pissed one of us off enough, another was waiting in the wings. Still I hope he sorts himself out and finds happiness. I now know he was never the One or my soulmate. He was just a chapter.

I have always thought it ironic, weird even, that I have been so defined by the men that I have been out with, as they have had very little input in my life. I have never married any of them, and no one has given me a massive divorce payout or bought me a pair of fine houses to float around in. None of my relationships has ever advanced my career. Anything I have ever managed to achieve, earn, buy or produce I have done on my own. I have never asked anyone to pay any of my bills, my credit cards or my debts. In fact, a lot of the time I have ended up having to fork out for other people.

After Thom left and my reconciliation with Danny

failed, I was beginning to think that perhaps I was better off on my own. I didn't need a bloke, a boyfriend or a husband to feel complete. I was perfectly happy to be single. From then on I decided I wasn't going to look for love any more. Everyone knows you should never go looking for it, because if you look, you will never find it.

As D. H. Lawrence once said, 'Those that go searching for love only make manifest their own lovelessness, and the loveless never find love, only the loving find love, and they never have to seek for it.'

10

Brand Brook

Almost every day there are paparazzi outside my house. I spoke to one of them the other day as he was running backwards down the street, with his lens in my face, just as I was popping round the corner in some Lululemon leggings trying to buy a sandwich. He was exhausted: he'd been on the 'Kelly Brook shift from 3 p.m. to 6 p.m.'. I had no idea I was an actual 'shift', but there you go! All he really wanted to do was take a few snaps and go home. Don't get me wrong, they are not permanently outside my house twenty-four hours a day, but when a situation arises – I'm dating someone, someone's been cheating on me, or I've been fired by Simon Cowell – then they'll set up camp outside and run backwards down the street until they get the shots they want. I gave the man a smile, so he could get what he wanted and go home, and I could carry on and buy my cheese sandwich.

My motto when face to face with Fleet Street's finest is: no matter what's happening, just smile. Just look 'dumb and fun'. Even if they are falling over themselves trying to take your photo in some sort of pap pile-up in the street, never look shocked, never look cross, irritated or annoyed. Otherwise that's the picture they'll use. So smile like you love it, stay dumb and fun. It is the perfect pap-face.

The selfie face is slightly different. To get a reasonably good selfie takes practice. There's the 'chin down' or the 'chin up' look. Obviously you have to smize with your eyes – look like you've a vicious case of conjunctivitis and can barely stand the sunlight. Or there's my default selfie, the tilt: profile, with your chin down, showing your good side. My friend Preeya Kalidas does the same face, which is fine until the two of us are together, working the same look, and then it becomes a little #awkward!

I am not saying that press attention is entirely awful, because it's not, and I have certainly come a long way since posing with a hand bra in the *Daily Star*. In fact, one thing press attention has obviously done is given me a profile, and ironically with that comes freedom, freedom to realize some of my dreams and passions. And one of those was to get into the world of fashion.

Having been turned down by all those top fashion agencies in town at the tender age of sixteen, it was a particularly sweet moment when I was invited to be on the front cover of *Love* magazine and be photographed by the internationally renowned photographic duo Mert and Marcus. Katie Grand, the editor of the magazine, knew my sister, Sasha, back in the day, and it was incredibly flattering to join the short list of extremely glamorous women who had gone before me: Giselle, Lauren Hutton, Alessandra Ambrosia, Sienna Miller, Rosie Huntington-Whiteley. It was more exciting than being asked to do *Vogue* at the time because *Love* was so hot. And the photos were fabulous. I was nude but for a feather boa and it was extremely liberating.

In fact, 2010 was an amazing year in that respect. After I shot with Mert and Marcus, I walked for Giles Deacon at London Fashion Week in September. I also did a Gina shoes campaign with the extremely talented photographer Solve Sundsbo, and I shot a Giorgio Armani advert for a Kind of Blue perfume in a white wig with a large, heaving bosom, again with Solve and Katie Grand. Then I went to LA and wore Armani at the Golden Globes, and following that, I hopped off to New York to go to the shows in Fashion Week, where I signed with a big New York agency, One Management. It was an extraordinary six months or so, as I was also a *Playboy* cover girl and shot by Ellen von Unwerth; the whole thing was very flattering. Finally to be embraced by the fashion industry aged thirty was something I never expected or dreamed could possibly happen. But then I think over the years the industry itself has changed. You no longer have to be a pencil-thin beanpole to be taken seriously; people who are different, or curvy, or small and curvy, are beginning to get a bit more of a chance. That's if you have a strong look and they like you. Kate Upton, for example, is all over every magazine front cover at the moment, and who can forget Sophie Dahl's Opium advert, for example? It was stunning. She looked like some fabulous Tamara de Lempicka painting. It didn't matter that she was curvier than the average model. In fact, it was a positive advantage.

But 'a look' doesn't just happen. It takes graft to keep it exciting and edgy. I am now thirty-four years old and I could look old and frumpy and not relevant very quickly, so for me, it is all about aligning myself with someone who will see me in a fresh way and photo-graph me like I have not been photographed before. This is where Madonna is fantastic. She is brilliant at finding people who see her differently. She has an incredible nose for talent and reinvention, and she keeps herself totally up to date about who is exciting, interesting and coming through. She is like a highly sen-sitive cultural weathervane. And in order to remain current, I need to keep my finger on the pulse and find people who will photograph me differently. I spend a lot of time researching, looking at editorial, looking at good advertising campaigns, looking for good people, looking for who's doing interesting stuff, the exciting stuff. I have a very good stylist, a twentysomething friend of mine called Kyle De'volle, who is always teasing me and accusing me of 'sucking the youth out of him', or 'sucking the youth out of his brain'. And I suppose he is right.

I really like the work of Damon Baker at the moment. He is only twenty-one and I first noticed him after seeing some fabulous photographs he'd done of Cara Delevingne and Rita Ora. They were so fresh and original and so arresting I really wanted to work with him. So I begged New Look to use him for the 2014 lingerie and fashion campaign, as I thought he would make it all look fresh and young. It gives the brand so much more PR if the pictures are new, exciting and a little bit unpredictable. Since then Damon and I have become good friends, and he has shot me for Turkish *GQ* and a few other publications.

In fact, the last shoot we did together I loved so much I asked if I could stay behind and do some nude shots. I am confident in my body, but I am even more confident in him making me look good. I wouldn't let just anyone shoot me like that, but when you meet someone who is really good, who knows about composition and how to photograph you properly, they will make you look beautiful no matter what your body

253

shape is. It is like art. Nudes are amazing. I really love nude photography; I have a bit of a collection. However, I've never put pictures of myself up on the wall at home. I am always focusing on what's next and not what I have done. Maybe I will when I am older and am nostalgic for firmer things past! But not now.

What is interesting is how photography has changed since I have been in the business. When I started out, the photographer would first take a Polaroid, and everyone would gather round and have a look at the small picture, and then you'd say, 'That's OK,' or, 'I might need a bit more hair here or eyeliner there.' Only when everything looked OK on the Polaroid would he take the real photograph. But now you jump straight in and it all comes up on a massive computer screen in the studio and it looks horrendous. Also, a lot of photographers these days don't know how to light their images properly because it is all done in post-production, so it can be very disheartening to view your poorly posed, un-retouched image on wide screen!

I admit I fight tooth and nail to work with the best people I can, and it is not easy. I am not a fashion model, nor am I an A-list movie star. I always strive to make my photo shoots better, as everyone else wants to do things as cheaply as they can and that is not the way to do it. It is a simple truth that you have to keep pushing boundaries to stay relevant. If you are irrelevant, obviously, no one cares.

And being seen in the right places helps. Part of my job is going out. Going out is work. Not out on the town with my friends, of course, but going to awards ceremonies, fashion-magazine parties, film festivals, that sort of thing. Does it make a difference for me to be seen in the right places, with the right people, at the right time? A hundred per cent it does. However, going out costs a small fortune!

Take the Cannes Film Festival, for example. It is hard work. You've got the red carpet, press junkets and daytime events where you are going to be photographed, and then you have to wear something else fabulous in the evening. It all comes out of your pocket at the end of the day, and it really adds up. You've got to have the right clothes and look great, otherwise there is no point in being there. So you have a stylist to help you pick out the clothes, and a make-up artist so you don't look like a fright. You need a hairdresser to get rid of the bedhead. You need your nails done, hair extensions, eyelash extensions, a spray tan. You need to book a hotel room, as you need somewhere to get everyone together to perform their magic. A car. A driver. Shoes. A bag. Some jewellery. And then, as you hit the red carpet after hours of being tonged, tweaked and painted, it's got to look graceful, effortless, on trend and easy. You're not allowed to sweat, look nervous, have a VPL, crusty feet, any armpit hair, snot coming out of your nose or spinach in your teeth. And then you're taken apart. Either by someone like Kelly Osbourne, who eviscerates you, live, from the cosy confines of her studio, or later on by the fashion press. You can spend thousands of pounds and still end up on the worst-dressed list. It's ridiculous! Or one flashbulb goes off and your pants are on show because you didn't realize the dress was transparent.

Normally I photograph myself from as many angles as possible to make sure it looks OK, there is nothing sticking out, and nothing embarrassing going on. However, I clearly failed to do that at last year's National TV Awards, when I was nominated for *Celebrity Juice* along with Leigh Francis, Fearne Cotton and Holly Willoughby. My vintage Ossie Clark wrap-dress went see-through under the strong flashes. Going bra-less that night was something of an error. Who would have thought to test the transparency of black silk jersey? Clearly not me! But as they say, there's no such thing as bad publicity.

As well as, hopefully, making sure an outfit is pap-proof, I will also photograph the whole lot together along with the shoes and the bag and so on. If you are on a promotional tour and you're doing interviews on *Jonathan Ross*, *This Morning*, plus breakfast news, you can get through six outfits in a day, and for simplicity and efficiency, you need to know what they look like. You need to know what earrings go with what dress, what goes with what shoes. Usually I put together a little look book. But then sometimes, when you've absolutely had it and can't cope with all the preening, you shove on a Primark jumpsuit and some old YSL heels and you look great.

I never drink at promotional events. I am not there to have fun. Obviously, sometimes they are fun, and it's great to catch up with old mates and colleagues, but it is essentially work. Sitting on the New Look table at the British Fashion Awards is entertaining, and I love everyone involved in the company, but I am there in my role as ambassador for New Look. My job is to wear New Look to the party and to wear it well so that everyone gets the press coverage they want the next day. The last thing I want to do is knock back the cheap booze and stagger out plastered, tripping up on the red carpet. I try to live my life in moderation. Everything else is so hyped up, I try to control what I can control.

However, one thing I can't control is other people's perceptions of who I am, and sometimes the Kelly Brook brand gets confused with the real Kelly Parsons.

I remember a couple of years ago I was on holiday on the Italian island of Ischia. I'd been to the annual film festival and was taking a bit of time out when a friend of a friend called me and said there were some guys in

Saint-Tropez who were having a huge party and wanted
to fly me down.

This happens quite often. I am sure I get asked more
than most because I am well known as a glamour model.
I've been in *Playboy*; I sell calendars; I am probably
pretty high on the 'party girl list'. No matter what I try
and do day to day and how I try and earn different types
of living, I will always attract that kind of attention and
I will always be invited to those sorts of private parties
– a yacht party, a villa party or a weekend in Vegas; I am
on those sorts of people's radar. I just try and sidestep
the question, be polite and try to get myself out of the
situation without being rude.

Often it's not just women these extremely rich men
are after. They want celebrities around them and they'll
invite Oscar-winning Hollywood movie stars to come
on their yacht in Sydney, or wherever they might be. I
think the idea is that if they have famous people around
them, then they'll attract the girls. You'd be amazed
who accepts these offers. There are some women in
Hollywood, and some extremely well-known models,
who live with these blokes and then take them for as
much money as they can. That's how they maintain
their lifestyles. It is dangerous, because once you get
used to that sort of super-rich lifestyle, how do you go
back? You can't. But also I imagine the older you get,
the fewer invitations you receive, and the greater the

demands that are made. It is the law of diminishing returns.

A while back, my old friend Steve Bing and some pals decided to go to Vegas for the night to watch Lady Gaga in concert. Bizarrely, I'd also been invited to a club opening in Vegas later that same night by some rich men from the Far East. We all boarded Steve's private jet at his own eco-friendly jet hangar in Burbank, and when we arrived we met Lady Gaga and watched her show. We all had dinner, after which Steve suggested we fly home. And I thought, Why not? I have no desire to go to a club opening and have drinks with these blokes from the Far East who I have never met. So I got on the plane and flew back. Meanwhile, my manager, who was in the club with the Far Eastern guys, was asked where I was. He told them I had gone back to LA and was on the jet home. And then I started getting phone calls.

'They'll pay you fifty thousand dollars to fly back . . . A hundred thousand . . . A hundred and fifty thousand . . .'

It went up and up. It was like a game to them. How much will it cost to get Kelly back? What's her price? They kept on offering more money. Half of you is tempted and thinks what you could do with the cash, and the other half is appalled. Obviously I didn't go back. I just couldn't. It was all a little bit grubby.

Anyway, I thought I'd managed to bow out of the

Ischia phone invitation to the party in Saint-Tropez with a degree of grace and decorum. But then a job offer arrived some four months later via my agent for me to go and open a restaurant in the Middle East. I was busy performing *Forever Crazy* with those fabulous Crazy Horse girls at the South Bank, I was also moving house and was up to my eyeballs in packing cases and bubble wrap, so I declined the offer. But they were persistent; they changed the opening night of the restaurant to coincide with the end of the show and made their initial payment twice as attractive. It was a fairly standard opening of an envelope/restaurant/supermarket/village fete deal that anyone in the public eye gets offered all the time. It was a one-day photocall with minimal PR and I'd be back on the plane the following day. What wasn't to love?

A very good friend of mine was doing business in the Middle East at the time and I asked her to come along. Initially, there was nothing suspicious about the phone call or the restaurant I was opening, other than the head of security being ridiculously effusive. He kept on saying how grateful everyone was that I was there. How delighted they were that I had accepted their invitation. It was only later at the bar that night that the truth came out.

It turned out one of the sons of the businessman who'd organized the trip was a fan and he'd been the one to invite me to Saint-Tropez. So I repeated very politely that I didn't really accept personal invitations or attend personal functions; however, corporate events handled by my agent were fine. I have to say at this point I was a little nervous, as it suddenly dawned on me the whole restaurant opening, the whole contract, the flights, the PR, the whole shebang had simply been a ruse to get me over there. Not only that, but according to the security guard, they had been duped by a conman in Saint-Tropez four months before. They'd paid him some £300,000 after he'd claimed he knew me and could get me to come to their party. In the end, he'd hired a lookalike, who'd flown in and pretended to be me. I was horrified. Not only that there was a girl out there pretending to be me, but that these men had been targeted in that way.

The next morning, we were called by our fixer and invited to go to the nearby shopping mall. We had some time before our flight, so we agreed. I have to admit I went a little mad. Egged on quite heavily by my friend, it became immediately apparent that anything either of us so much as paused to look at would be purchased, no questions asked. I remember walking into Louboutin and almost emptying the shop of nearly every size-39 shoe they had. High on retail therapy and loaded down with expensive shopping, we got on the plane home, thanked them profusely for their hospitality and their generosity, never to see them again. Or so I thought.

Little did I know that my girlfriend who'd come with me on the trip stayed in contact with them. They were nice enough men, but it was clear one of them had a crush on me and I am never the sort to give someone false hope, so I had very much kept my distance. But my friend had not. Don't get me wrong, I can shop long and hard with the best of them, but this felt very much out of my league.

Two months later, my friend called and asked if she could come round because she had something for me. She turned up with an extraordinarily beautiful diamond bracelet. I was gobsmacked and a little taken aback. I said I didn't want anything to do with it, but she insisted it was a gift, with the receipt if I wanted to take it back, and that it was given unconditionally. It was so sparkly and pretty I could almost hear the devil himself whispering sweet nothings in my ear. I am embarrassed to say I did take the bracelet. I didn't know what to do with it exactly, so it stayed in the box and I never wore it. As she said, it was unconditional. I didn't thank anyone for it either. I did like the man who sent it and would have happily had dinner with him, or any of his family, as they were all very charming and kind.

And a couple of months later, I did. My girlfriend came back into town and this is when things went mad and completely out of control. I was newly single – Thom had flown to LA – so I really appreciated the big dinners out and the days spent shopping. But my friend, who was now staying in the same hotel as the family, took it to an extreme. She'd call me every day, and every day it was diamonds, dresses, coats and handbags. It was non-stop. I'd go to meet her in Harrods and be bought ten Alaïa dresses in one afternoon and then be taken downstairs to the De Beers counter to choose a little diamond something to go with them. It was all apparently still unconditional. They were using my friend to get to me, and to be fair to her, I was letting it happen.

After five days of hectic shopping, fine dining and nightclubbing, my friend rang me again. I was to meet the boys at a garage on Park Lane. As I walked into the glitzy showroom, they handed me the keys to a brand-new Bentley Mulsanne. It was silvery blue, with a cream leather interior, pop-down self-illuminating vanity mirrors, two TVs in the back and more Loro Piana cashmere blankets than you could shake a sheikh at. One last little gift, before they went home. I was absolutely stunned. I had no idea what to do. I had never been near such an expensive, plush, over-the-top car in my entire life.

I spent the next two weeks being driven around by Alan in my brand-new Bentley. I sat on the back seat, dressed in my Alaïa, wrapped up in a Fendi fur, dripping with De Beers diamonds – I looked like a hooker. What the hell was I playing at? What on earth was I doing? Who had I become?

While shooting *Trollied*, a TV show in Bristol, Ash Atalla, the writer and producer of the show and a good friend of mine, who also produced the BBC2 hit comedy *The Office*, made a comment that the new changes to my lifestyle, the car, the diamonds, the fur coat were perhaps not really 'on brand'.

'Anyone would think the nice, down-to-earth, smiling, kind Kelly had changed,' he said, adding that I looked like I had lost the plot.

And I had. I have to admit it felt so good, but it was so wrong!

There and then I called the head of the family's security and asked him to come and collect everything. And I meant everything. It wasn't mine and I really didn't think I should keep it any more. I got a call back immediately saying that just because I couldn't afford nice things didn't mean I shouldn't have them, which was very kind and sweet, but I was insistent. I wanted to feel clean and I didn't.

Returning to London, my last journey in the Bentley, I remember sitting in the back of the car with a girlfriend and cracking open a bottle of Hendrick's gin, sipping it out of plastic cups. I love Hendrick's gin with a slice of cucumber, and together we got properly smashed. By the time we reached London, I'd lost £20 on the slots at Leigh Delamere services and had my head hanging out of the window about to be violently ill. As my friend tucked me into bed, I mumbled about how much I loved that car and how much Alaïa really did suit me. She said, 'Don't worry, Kel, it'll be fine. Well done for giving it all back. Just think, it's a good chapter for the book.'

So there you are. Half a chapter! My *Pretty Woman* dream turned sour! I had overstepped the line and learned my lesson.

Usually when blokes try and overstep the line, it's just like dealing with a bunch of naughty little boys. Most of the time I feel in control of it and it doesn't really bother me. I am thirty-four. I can handle myself. I got through being a glamour model without being touched up. I would just leave if anything ever looked like it might get out of control. But I do like men, and I do like that banter. If they whistle when I walk past a building site, I don't particularly care. I am not insulted. I think most of these guys are smart enough to know what they can get away with. I have never felt in a position where things have gone too far. I have never been raped or molested. I have never been in a situation where someone has thought they were going to get something from me and they've become upset because they haven't got it. I never promise something I can't deliver. I grew up in a pub; I became used to that banter. My dad was a scaffolder, and my mother had a smart, sharp tongue. I learned to handle myself very young. I have never really been naive. My pap-face may be 'dumb and fun', but I am certainly not.

I have a sound business head on my shoulders and am well aware that not everyone is going to keep looking at me in my underwear for the rest of my life! I know I have to diversify, take stock and move on. If I could be photographed in a bikini for the rest of my life, I would, because it is fun and I enjoy it. I am quite an exhibitionist, and I like looking sexy. But I am also enjoying diversifying.

Recently I joined forces with Nick House to open a fantastic late-night cocktail bar and Americana restaurant, Steam & Rye, in Leadenhall Street, London. Nick has had huge success with clubs like Mahiki and Whisky Mist, and I knew him from the olden days with Piers Adam and Guy Ritchie. It is a great, fun place with good food and delicious cocktails. My job is to talk about it and promote it. I don't have to go there every week or every month, under contract, but I try and go as often as I can, as I actually really love the place. I think my association is supposed to give it a PR boost. Nick wanted to tap into the City and the East London crew. He is extremely well known in Mayfair and Kensington, and he thought I might help him to go east, as it were.

Launch night was great, even though I did have a few issues with the car. First of all, the doorbell rang, which, take it from me, is always a bad sign. You see, a chauffeur never rings the doorbell. A chauffeur never calls; they wait until you are ready. They sit and wait because they are polite. You know it is a rubbish car when they ring the bell or sound the horn. So I asked my mate Michael to check what car the PR company had sent, saying, 'Darling, I know it is a Prius, just by the sound of the doorbell.'

Two minutes later, he came back. 'Darling,' he replied, 'you're right!'

'We're not getting into a Prius!' I flounced, and promptly booked an Uber.

I might sound spoilt, but you can't have a big event, get dressed up and arrive in a Prius. For a start, we couldn't fit all five of us in, and it doesn't look good – it destroys the artifice and the illusion. Surely the PR people should know that. The press, who were all gathered outside my flat at the time, laughed and said, 'I can't believe you didn't get into that car, Kelly! What are you like?'

But you have to look the part when you're publicizing something. I don't care what car I drive normally – I couldn't give a damn – but when you are working or turning up somewhere, you have to do it properly. You have to play the game. It's business.

Anyway, the bar continues to do really well. We have a great chef, amazing cocktails, including the very popular Monica Lewinsky, and a mechanical rodeo bull, which arrived from Louisiana just after Christmas and goes down a storm with the City boys.

Is it something I'd like to do again? I love being a part of it all, but bars and clubs are not entirely my bag. I like having a drink, but I am much more into health and fitness these days. And it was one of the reasons why I decided to move back to LA. LA is far more health-conscious – it reeks of kale juice and workout gear – and to have any sort of longevity in what I do, I have to look after myself. I can't keep knocking back the cocktails; it's not good for me! Thankfully, there is not much to tempt you in LA. It is an industry town; all you do is work, or work out, or talk about working out and worry why you're not working!

So in January 2014, I moved back to LA. Just before I arrived, I did a quick swimwear shoot in Miami for New Look, and then stayed on to shoot my calendar. My calendar is a Brand Brook staple. I have produced one a year every year since 2001. I will try and use the best photographer and stylist I can, and together with my team at ROAR we will try and come up with an interesting concept. We'll then shoot the hell out of it for a few days, including making a behind-the-scenes viral video, and will syndicate the pictures internationally to *FHM*, *Maxim*, the tabloids, and the weeklies like *Nuts* and *Zoo*, which are still incredibly popular. It is great to reach such a wide audience and still have control over the pictures they are using.

So then, after a few days in Miami, it was straight to LA, where I have rented a pretty art deco apartment just off Sunset Boulevard, which used to be the home of Marilyn Monroe and is where she stayed shortly after splitting up with Joe DiMaggio. It was initially rather strange to be back in LA, as I have quite a history there now, and have had so many different lives in the city. But for once it was entirely on my own terms. I could decorate my flat how I wanted; I could make it as girlie and as pretty as I fancied. And I have to say some of the old haunts do still hold their charm. I defy anyone to find better, more delicious, more succulent or more opulent cakes than at Sweet Lady Jane on Melrose.

Every time I go in there, which is frankly probably a little more often than I should, I'm reminded of the ridiculously delicious and enormous cake I asked them to made for Billy's fortieth birthday. Based on the one true love of his life, an old Mustang he'd had since the age of eighteen, the cake was pale blue and must have been about two feet long. It was phenomenal. As indeed was the party. I remember hiring the Silent Movie Theatre in LA, where the idea was for everyone to have a huge custard-pie fight. One of Billy's favourite film scenes was the pie fight in *The Great Race*, starring Tony Curtis. I planned the whole thing meticulously. I even called Tony Curtis's agent and asked if he could come to the party to pie Billy in the face. Sadly, Mr Curtis was in Vegas, but the rest of the evening came off beautifully and ended in a massive pie fight. It was one of the best and certainly one of the most expensive nights of my life! I made such an effort that evening. But it was an important birthday; I was hardly going to say, 'Let's go for a Nando's on your fortieth.' Which, interestingly, was how Danny 'treated me' on my thirtieth: I went to Nando's and had a lemon chicken and herb wrap. I threw a huge party for Billy on his fortieth and then there I was on my thirtieth having a Nando's in Wimbledon. How did that happen?

It is all, as they say, water under the bridge. But what is interesting is how the past somehow always finds a way of catching up with you.

The 2nd March 2014 was Oscar night, which is one of the most fabulously fun nights in LA, when anyone and everyone puts on their glad rags and parties. I had a few invitations for various events but had decided to go to Elton John's hugely glamorous party, which he holds to raise money for his AIDS charity, and then I thought I might pop in to Mike De Luca's on the way home. He's the Oscar-nominated producer of *The Social Network* and is currently producing *Fifty Shades of Grey*. His party was rumoured to be rocking and going on long into the night.

Obviously, I needed a frock, plus hair and make-up, and who better to ask than my old mates: Suzie, Sadie's sister, who is a couturier and who has made me fabulous dresses for numerous parties and red-carpet events in the past, and Gary Cockerill.

Gary arrived at my apartment just as the first statues were being handed out and I'd opened a cold bottle of pink champagne. (Well, it was Oscar night.) Accompanied by a large wheelie suitcase full of make-up and with his roll of brushes under his arm, he was dressed in a white shirt and jeans with a thick crop of blond hair and was a little stressed. He'd been on the go since that morning and I was his fourth or fifth client of the day. We had kept in touch with each other since the Jeany Savage days, sixteen years ago. Gary regularly comes round to my flat, or we'll go out for dinner and have a few cocktails now and then, but it had been a long while since I'd had my face 'Gary-ed', as my old mates used to say.

'Right,' he said, setting out his brushes and powders all over my dining-room table, 'I am going to make you look fabulous and sexy and gorgeous – the usual. Is that OK? It's a different job from what it used to be,' he continued, narrowing his eyes and inspecting me closely. 'In the old days, I used to have to paint a face on you, as you didn't really have one. Well, you did, but it was all round, a little girl's face, and I used to have to colour in those contours to give you some bones. Now you have the face of a woman, it is a totally different job.'

'Are you trying to tell me I've aged?' I asked him.

'For the better,' he replied. 'For the very much better. Your nose has got smaller! I remember having to take the sides off it, and of course you had no eyebrows at all because your mum had plucked the shit out of them! I used to spend hours trying to draw them in!' he laughed.

There's something very relaxing about seeing someone you've known your entire adult life. It's a privilege to have close friends, particularly in this fickle and ephemeral business.

'You haven't changed a bit, Gary,' I mumbled, as he grabbed hold of my chin and started to get to work.

'You have,' he grinned. 'Do you remember the chamois leather bikini?'

'How could I forget! D'you remember Marcella went and got the leathers from the local garage round the corner and cobbled the whole thing together!'

Along with the gossip and the sips of pink bubbles, it took Gary about an hour to work his magic – the hair, the lashes, the plumped-up lips. In the end, he couldn't resist a little bit of contouring. The result was impressive. Bearing in mind I had a stinking bout of flu at the time, I looked more than ready for any red carpet. Then my other old friend Suzie turned up with an elegant, understated, black floor-length fitted dress that she'd designed herself. It was perfect. Teamed with some diamonds and pearls plus a little fur shrug, I was ready to go.

Finally, as the last of the pink Perrier-Jouët disappeared and the Uber cab pulled up outside the building, it was time to leave. Who knew what the night had in store for us? Who knew where we'd end up and who we'd meet? But if there is one thing that I have always loved about LA, one thing that makes it special, it's that your luck can change in a moment; the wheel of fortune can suddenly turn. Anything is possible . . .

11

One Big, Happy Beginning

I was in my house in Kent when I got 'the call'.

Pilot season had been surprisingly slow. I'd been hanging out in LA for about six weeks and had grown quite bored of going to the gym and walking around clutching a kale and parsley juice, waiting for the phone to ring, so I'd decided to go back to the UK. I was launching a fragrance, Audition, and was in talks with Simply Be about a clothing line and had been asked to contribute to some design meetings with them. So I had plenty to do on the other side of the Pond.

It was the weekend of 14 March 2014. I was at my farmhouse, hanging out with my little brother and catching up on the last couple of months of gossip, when suddenly an email arrived from my agent in LA. Attached was an amazing half-hour script for a sitcom in the vein of *Seinfeld* and *Friends*.

It was extraordinary. It was just what I wanted to do.

I'd had an honest conversation with my agent before I left LA saying that comedy was what I really wanted to focus on. I'd been following the career of Sofia Vergara from *Modern Family* because my agent represented her as well, and had used her as an example, telling me not to give up hope. Like me, she was a glamour girl famous for modelling bikinis, and had got her break quite late in her career. And what a break! There is something magical about that alchemy of the right role at the right time that can really catapult you to a different level. So despite all the knockbacks, I'd never given up on the hope that it could happen for me, and more proactively, I had decided to really put it out there that that's what I wanted to do.

And there it was. The script. They actively wanted a British actress for the three-handed show. It was to be produced by Ellen DeGeneres and written by Liz Feldman, who was responsible for *2 Broke Girls*, which is a massive show on CBS. The pilot was called *One Big Happy* and was the story of a bloke and his lesbian best friend, who find themselves still single in their thirties and living together, and so decide to have a baby with each other, as no one else better had come along. Having tried to get pregnant for a while without success, one night the bloke (played by Nick Zano) meets a wild and naughty English girl in a bar and falls madly in love. They decide to go to Vegas together to get married, only to return to the flat to find out that the lesbian best friend (played by Elisha Cuthbert) has actually finally fallen pregnant. The story continues with how these three misfits work it out and decide to bring up the baby together.

The show was very now, about dysfunctional families, with a whiff of *Will & Grace*, and I don't think there had been a sitcom centred around a gay woman on US TV really since Ellen herself, all those years ago in the eponymous TV show in which she'd starred. Ellen had also just presented the Oscars a couple of weeks previously, with Liz writing for her, so I could not have been in better company.

It was also with Warner Brothers, with whom I'd made *Smallville*, so I was familiar with the studio. To say I was excited was an obvious understatement. But equally, I knew none of this would amount to anything if the show was not picked up. You can spend millions and months on a pilot and it can go nowhere.

I immediately asked my brother to help me learn my lines. We read the script together. He played all the other characters; he is not an actor at all, but he was very patient. He went over and over it with me again and again.

On the Thursday, I drove up to London and had two auditions that day, one for *Plebs*, an ITV2 show about young citizens of Rome, and the other for *One Big Happy*. They wanted me to record my performance on tape and send it to Ellen and Portia de Rossi. The next day, I got the call to say I'd got the job on *Plebs*, which I was thrilled about, but before I accepted it I wanted to wait to see if *One Big Happy* would come off as the dates would clash. So I waited out the weekend. I launched my perfume, Audition, in Manchester, which was hugely successful, staying there with a friend.

On the Monday morning, I woke to an email from my agents asking where on earth I was and informing me that I had to be in LA by 11 a.m. the next day. They wanted to test me immediately. I had less than twenty-four hours to get from Manchester to LA and I didn't even have my passport on me. I called Damian in Kent and asked him to meet me at Heathrow with my passport, so I could fly to LA via New York. Then I went to Manchester Piccadilly Station only to find that there were delays on the line. I couldn't risk the possibility of being kicked off the train and getting stuck in the middle of nowhere unable to get anywhere; it wasn't worth it. So my friend offered to drive. We got to London in record time, where I met my brother, grabbed my passport and got straight on the flight to New York with just the clothes I stood up in and my handbag.

I arrived in New York at 2 a.m., slept for four hours in a terrible airport motel and then got the first flight out to LA. I arrived just in time to go through the script with Warner Loughlin, my acting coach, trying to find extra beats and laughs in the script, and then I went straight into Warner Brothers, where I met Liz Feldman and the producers, Portia de Rossi and Jeff Kleeman, and the other two girls I was up against.

I honestly think sometimes that the acting and the filming are the easy bit; what is actually hard is the investment of time, energy and money, constantly putting yourself out there only to be knocked back. The job itself I love so much I'd do it for free, but the process is knackering and thankless.

The other girls were in the same position. One had been in a hotel for a week on her own in LA. She didn't know anyone; she couldn't drive; she'd just been told she couldn't go home. She'd been tested three times already and they were not prepared to give her the role until they had exhausted all other options. That's how cruel this business is. It has happened to me many times.

After about half an hour of nerves and tension waiting to be called in, I read for the role and it wasn't too bad. All those other auditions, the knockbacks, the days yelling down the mike at *The Big Breakfast* held me in good stead. Although my audition didn't pass without 'notes'. After I read with Nick Zano and Elisha Cuthbert – the two stars who'd already been cast for the show – they rang up my agent and said they liked what I was doing, but I had hair 'straight out of a beauty pageant'.

That morning, out of nervous energy and by way of compensating for my Phileas Fogg of a journey, I had chucked my hair in rollers and bouffed the hell out of it. So they asked me to come back to audition for the network in high heels, not the boots I was wearing, and with more 'natural' hair.

The next day, it was the network auditions. Peter Roth, the head of the studio, was in the middle of the room, and there were rows of producers and execs either side of him, all sitting in some complicated, heavily nuanced hierarchy that only a third-generation Hollywoodite would have understood.

The audition itself was also a test of our chemistry. The girl who went in before me came out rather flushed and said, 'Oh my God, you've got to kiss him!'

Normally you'd have a few more meetings with the other actor before you got to tongues, and to be honest, I wasn't really prepared for a full-on kissing scene. But I thought, It's between the three of us, and I suppose they do really need to see if there is any chemistry between us. So poor Nick Zano really got it. I launched myself at him and wrapped my leg round him like a serpent. There was no point in holding back! I ate his face off. I had to go for it. I couldn't be shy. It was very weird. I looked at him and thought, Let's do this!

Sometimes these things are just meant to be. I got the role. They said they'd been looking for the right person for that role for months. They'd tested hundreds of actresses and no one had quite hit the sweet spot. It had been like 'trying to find a magical unicorn', or so they said. It was only down to Steven Salisbury that I ever went up for the part in the first place. He was an assistant at Untitled, my agents, and had found the script in a pile right at the end of pilot season, after everyone else had looked at it and passed, and he thought I might be OK at it. He has since been promoted from assistant to agent.

I didn't really have much chance to think about, or appreciate, the fact that I had got the role, because the following day was the full read-through. It took place in a vast studio with a great long table laid with place names and bottles of water. This was the first time the network and the studio had seen the whole cast together. You can be recast at this point if you don't work. Fortunately, no one told me this! At read-throughs they make notes about stories, plots, jokes and characters, and this is when they start to make huge changes and really hone the script ready to shoot the pilot. It was extremely exciting, and thankfully went well. I should have been exhausted, but I wasn't. The adrenalin was really keeping me going.

A week later, I started rehearsals. It was like a dream come true. Driving to Warner Brothers, going onto the lot with your pass, parking in your own spot, walking to your own dressing room with your name on the door and being handed your script with your lines already highlighted; it is the sort of thing you fantasize about. It was a whole different level.

We filmed on Stage 18, which is supposed to be a lucky stage. *Casablanca* was filmed there, as was *A Streetcar Named Desire*, *The West Wing* and *Gilmore Girls*. During breaks you can drive around the set and find yourself in New York; then on the other side of the road, it's Chicago! The whole place is steeped in history. The sets are incredible and are permanent.

I didn't meet Ellen for the first week and a half. She films *The Ellen DeGeneres Show* on the next-door stage, and Portia de Rossi, her wife and one of the producers, was on set every day reporting back to her, so she was very much in the loop and always around, but I just hadn't met her yet.

Ten days into filming, I had a nude scene, and because *One Big Happy* is for a network channel and not cable, this was a big deal. Nudity is much more normal on something like *Game of Thrones*, but it is rare on the networks, so there was a huge amount of discussion as to how they were going to shoot it. Elisha's character, the uptight lesbian, finds my character, Prudence, who is very much a fun free spirit in touch with her body, totally starkers after she has stayed over. Ellen said that originally everyone was going to expect the lesbian character to be all over my character, but she really doesn't find me at all attractive. It is basically making the point that not all lesbians fancy all girls.

Anyway, it was a closed set and there I was rehearsing, standing with pasties – flesh-coloured plasters – over my boobs and my bits. Suddenly Ellen walked into the room. Apparently she loves a practical joke, but I screamed so loudly when I saw her! I was shocked. I didn't expect to meet her in nothing but pasties. She just laughed and said, 'Where am I in this scene?'

She did it on purpose! She is so naughty. I met her later that day and she made the inevitable joke – 'Hi, Kelly. I didn't recognize you with your clothes on!'

But she was so supportive. She told me that making the show would be like having a baby. Some days it would be so painful and awful and I'd be tearing my hair out over the fact that it was all so stressful, and other days I was going to love it. She said that in the end we'd deliver something that was amazing and would make us all so happy.

She was right that it was a gruelling process, but she was so helpful, as she really knew what it was like. She'd give us all ten-minute pep talks to keep us motivated. I think Elisha was the one under the most pressure, as she was playing the lesbian character. Ellen, Portia and Liz are leading lesbians in Hollywood, real role models, and she was the one representing their sexuality.

The rehearsals lasted two weeks. Then we did a pre-shoot, which was all the naked footage, and then we shot in front of a studio audience, which was like acting on steroids. There was a crazy energy about it. I remember asking Liz how many goes I'd get.

'You get one,' she replied. 'Possibly two. But no more. The audience've heard it already – they are not going to laugh at the same joke twice.'

It was like being a stand-up. Except worse. You're dealing with props, the stage, moving around and other actors who have either learned or not learned their lines. There is a lot that can go wrong. Even if you have learned your lines, you have to be prepared to drop the script and read something else at a moment's notice. If something doesn't work with the audience, the writers or one of the producers will walk on stage, change the line and say, 'Try this.'

We tore through the script, literally. Elisha ripped every page out of the script as soon as we shot it. That sort of energy gives everything such incredible momentum. The next day, I woke up and I'd hit a brick wall. The last time I'd felt that exhausted was after *Strictly Come Dancing*. There is something about performing live that drains you like nothing else. It is all the adrenalin. I lay in bed and did not move for a whole day. When you have experienced performing at that level, there is nothing else like it. I imagine it is the closest actors get to being rock stars, and I imagine that's why rock stars do it. It is one hell of a ride. It is not like making a film, when you sit in your trailer for eight out of the sixteen hours of your day. With this type of TV, you're on, and you stay on until you're finished, often quite literally.

We all then disappeared off to the Coachella music festival for the weekend – Elisha, Liz and her wife, who wrote the theme tune for the show. It was fabulous. We rented a house and had a great time. We all had to forget about the show now; it was no longer in our hands. We had given it our best shot and could do nothing more now except hope and pray that it would be commissioned.

It is all such a lottery, if a show gets picked up or not, and who knows why some make it and some don't? All I could think was that it was such an amazing experience. I forced myself not to think about the rest. Just in case there was no rest. So I blocked out any hope or aspiration and forgot about it until 12 May, which is the day that NBC announces its autumn schedule. We were up against fifteen other comedies. They had a shortlist of sixteen, but over a hundred had been submitted originally. It is all so highly competitive it doesn't bear thinking about.

A few weeks after the shoot, I had dinner with Liz, who had just seen the final edit of the show. I was desperate to see it, hear about it, anything. I begged and grovelled, but she was having none of it. She refused point blank. It was all so secretive. I plied her with as much wine as I could, but she stuck to her guns. All she could tell me was that it was testing well with audiences across the States and that one supersized lady in the South had put up her hand after a screening and said, 'I relate to Prudence.'

So far so good.

I flew back to Kent to wait it out. I had no idea what the final show looked like or how I had done. It was out of my hands and in the lap of the gods, or more precisely, in the lap of the NBC executives.

But there are times when you feel that a project is right and there are no bad eggs in the omelette, and this felt right. I loved everyone I was working with. I loved the show. We all got on. I just had to cross my fingers and wait.

By Friday 9 May I had still heard nothing, so I decided to go to a pub for supper with my girlfriend, Jo. There was no mobile-phone reception there, and when I got home and checked my phone, I saw I had about fifteen missed calls and messages, all saying things like 'Woo-hoo – you've done it!' and 'Well done! I can't believe it!'

NBC had picked up the show and I was due in New

York two days later to go to what is more commonly known as the 'up fronts'.

I loaded up my car, drove to London, had dinner with my cousin Sally and got on the plane the next day. I landed in New York, checked into the Ritz-Carlton, popped on a red McQueen dress that I'd bought, without even trying on, in Selfridges the day before and went off to meet the whole of NBC.

I walked into a conference-centre room to shouts of congratulations and was introduced to Minnie Driver, Anna Friel, Debra Messing and the cast of *Chicago Fire*. It was extraordinary. Everyone was in the same boat: they'd all made pilots and they had all been picked up. The atmosphere was incredible. Electric. All you can ever hope for is to be invited to the table to have a shot at it. And this was it. My shot. I now have to make six great shows and hope that they work. If they do, fantastic. If not, what a great experience!

What a ride! And this is just the beginning . . .

Picture Acknowledgements

All photographs are from the author's private collection apart from:

Page 4, bottom: © Richard Blower

Page 6, top left and right: © Local World

Page 6, bottom: © Jeany Savage/Express Syndication

Page 7: © Jeany Savage/Express Syndication

Page 8, right: © Doug Peters/EMPICS Entertainment

Page 9, bottom: Neil Munns/PA Archive/Press Association Images

Page 10, middle: © REX/RICHARD YOUNG

Page 10, bottom: © REX

Page 12, top: Dancing with Jason © REX/RICHARD YOUNG

Page 13, middle: © REX/c.showtime/Everett

Page 14, bottom: © REX/ITV

Page 15, top right: © Getty Images

Page 16: Photograph by Benjamin Kaufmann, © Kelly Brook

Page 18: © BBC

Page 19, bottom: © REX/Ken McKay

Page 20, top: © REX/Nikos Vinieratos

Page 22, top right: © Dean Freeman

Page 23, top right: © REX/David Fisher

Page 23, bottom: © WireImage

Page 24: © Neil Stewart c/o We Folk